BLUEPRINT FOR WRITING SUCCESS

Also by Sherry Peters

Non-Fiction
Silencing Your Inner Saboteur

Fiction
Mabel the Lovelorn Dwarf
Mabel the Mafioso Dwarf

BLUEPRINT FOR WRITING SUCCESS

SHERRY PETERS

© 2015 Sherry Peters

All rights reserved. No portion of this book may be reproduced by any process or technique without the express consent of the author, except in the case of brief quotations embodied in critical articles and reviews.

DwarvenAmazon Press
www.dwarvenamazon.com

Printed in the U.S.A.

Peters, Sherry, 1973 -
Blueprint for Writing Success

Print ISBN: 978-0-9920535-5-0
Ebook ISBN: 978-0-9920535-6-7

Cover images:
© Christopherhall | Dreamstime.com - Books Photo
© Fontgraf | Dreamstime.com - Graph Paper For Building And Architectural Drawings Photo
:

For
Gerald Brandt

CONTENTS

Acknowledgements — 9

Introduction — 11

The Foundation — 19
    Setting the Foundation — 20
        No Guarantees
        Know Why You Write
        Why Are You Writing This Story?
        Place And Space
        Setting A Routine
        Keep Your Eyes On The Prize
        Support System

First Floor: Dreaming Big — 39
    Free Your Mind — 42
    What's Stopping You? — 44
        Fear Of Failure
        Fear Of Not Being Good Enough
        Fear Of Rejection
        Fear Of Not Being Original
        Fearing No One Will Want To Read Your Work
    The Satisfaction Equation   60
    Luck Favours The Prepared   64

Second Floor: Getting to Work — 69
    Getting to Work — 71
    Time, Priorities, and Goals, Oh My! — 73
    The Writing Process — 89
        Pantsing
        Plotting
        Linear
        Random
        Multitasking
    The Writing — 95

Third Floor: The Murky Middle and Beyond — 101
    The Murky Middle — 103
        Fear of Upsetting People
        Fear of Conflict
    Connecting with Our Core Values — 109
    Getting Feedback — 114

Fourth Floor: Going Public — 119
    Indie v. Tradition Publishing — 121
    Marketing — 126
    Fear of Rejection / Fear of Success — 127

Rooftop Garden: Celebrate! — 129

Final Thoughts — 133

Journal Questions — 139
    Foundation
    Dreaming Big
    Getting to Work
    The Murky Middle
    And Beyond
    Going Public
    Celebrate!

Worksheets — 187
    Internal/External Reference
    Time Log
    Life Balance Wheel
    Prioritization
    Goal Setting
    Timeline

About the Author — 207

ACKNOWLEDGEMENTS

Many thanks to my coaching instructors and classmates, my clients, and workshop attendees. Thank you to my family for their patience with me as I continually abandon them for my pursuit of this writing thing in all its forms. Thank you to all my writing friends. I couldn't do this without your support and your belief in me. Thank you also and always to my best friends Adria Laycraft, Gerald Brandt, and Robert J. Sawyer.

INTRODUCTION

INTRODUCTION

There is no magical trick to writing a book, story, screenplay, or poem. Yes, there are elements of the craft of writing to learn, like plot, character and description that should be developed along the way. But if you simply want to write, the only thing you need to do, is sit down and put one word after another on the page. Writing isn't hard. Persisting at it, completing a story, pursuing a career as a writer is hard. When most of us start writing, we don't think about the time commitment needed the murky middle of the story when we get bored, the distractions, the rejection, or what happens next. When you're starting out as a writer, you don't need to think about those things. If you want to be a writer, an author, you need to think about those things.

If you've been writing for any length of time, you know all the distractions and self-doubt that can and does, get in our way. It doesn't have to be that way. You can structure your writing process, time, and career, so that you *can* succeed.

Unfortunately, in writing, there are no guarantees that what you write will sell, or be a bestseller. For our purposes, we will define success as completing your writing projects, submitting or publishing, writing more projects, and pursuing a career as an author so that your work does sell.

With this *Blueprint for Writing Success*, you can plan and prepare for each stage of the process of writing each project. You can plan to succeed by anticipating the work ahead, and prepare yourself for the inevitable distractions and pitfalls so that you can get past them. This blueprint will look at building the foundation, planning, getting to work, the murky middle, and going public. Each stage will cover the process, what to expect, what gets in the way, and tools to succeed. The best part about this blueprint, is that it can be tweaked and perfected as each writing project dictates.

As a Writing Success Coach, I have worked with writers just starting out putting their first words on the page, writers who have one or two books out or under contract, and writers who are well established on the bookstore shelves. Every tool, every question in this book, I have used with my clients to help them find their own writing success. If you'd like to know what they have to say about the process, you can read their testimonials on my website at: http://www.sherrypeters.com/coaching/testimonials.

More importantly, I am also a writer. I have been in the game a long time. Just like you, I have struggled to get the words on the page. I have struggled with trying to write while having an emotionally and mentally draining job. I have the same fears as every other writer. I can be the Queen of Procrastination. Devastating rejections have stopped me from writing for a couple of months, but they have also made me be more determined than ever to dive back in and prove them wrong. I have found relief from the day job in my writing. I have learned to embrace my fears of failure and rejection, to use them as motivation to be better, to do more. I have stared my self-doubt in it's big, sickly-green, bulging eyes, and defeated it.

What I have learned as a writer and a coach for writers, I have put down on these pages.

What's Inside

Before I get into what you will find inside this book and how to use the tools provided, I want to define a few of the terms I use, which may not be exactly the same as what you are used to.

The first term is *Success*. I've already mentioned it above, but it is worth re-stating. For the purposes of this book, I am talking about only the elements of writing which are in our control, which is the writing itself. Therefore, I am defining success as a writer as: *getting the words on the page, polishing them up, sending them out, and writing more.* Simple as that.

The next term is *Career*. I'm going to talk a lot about your career as a writer, or having a writing career. What I am referring to here, is taking writing seriously enough to put time and effort into writing with the purposes of it being published. This isn't about being able to write full-time, or even necessarily earning a lot of money from it. Your career as a writer started the moment you decided you wanted to be an author and took steps towards making that happen.

I refer to *story, book, novel,* and *project* interchangeably. Some of you are writing short stories, some are writing novels. Maybe you write screenplays, and maybe you write poetry. Rather than naming each one every time I refer to your work-in-progress, I've chosen to refer to it as the story or project you're writing.

And finally, I will on occasion mention the *Inner Saboteur*. The Inner Saboteur is the voice of self-doubt and fear. It embodies the inner editor, censor, and critic. It is the voice that tells you it is OK to take an evening off from writing because you've had a difficult day at work and you deserve a treat. Your Inner Saboteur will do and say anything to stop you from writing. It wants you to fail.

Each section of this book will build on the tools of the previous section, much like designing a multi-storey building. At the end of the book you will find journal pages with space for you to work through the questions I have asked you. Some of the questions will seem repetitive, because they are. My hope is that as you go through this book, you will grow as a writer, and so will your dream for your writing career. You will also find a series of worksheets that I have referred to throughout the book. Additionally, both the journal pages and worksheets are available to download from my website http://www.sherrypeters.com/blueprintextras. Don't worry, I'll give you the web address again.

Here's how this will work. As we build our writing life around us, there will be many things that will try to destroy it; things like rejections, fear, and self-doubt. The first section of this book is all about building a solid foundation beneath us to withstand those threats, to catch us when we fall, and to provide something solid to build on from the start or re-build on should the upper floors crumble. The foundation includes knowing why you write, why you write what you write, creating habits to be able to write whenever you have a moment and wherever you are, and having strong support from family and friends.

From the foundation we'll move on to the first floor of Dreaming Big. This section is all about allowing your inner child to play, to free your creativity, and freedom for both your writing career and what stories you want to write. We're going to spend some time talking about what gets in the way, what stops us from being creative, from allowing ourselves to dream, what keeps us from putting the first words on the page. After we've talked about what stops us, we'll focus on ways to push past those obstacles.

Once we've accomplished the dreaming big, we'll talk about getting to work. This section is all about getting the words on the page. We'll cover time management, prioritization and goal setting. We'll also talk about the different kinds of writing processes so that you can find one that works best for you. We'll finish with covering the excuses we make as to why we can't write.

The third floor is the murky middle and beyond. This is the place in our writing where we start to lose faith in the story. The story starts to lag, and so does your motivation. The fear of upsetting people and the fear of conflict will be discussed. And then we'll focus on getting your motivation back so that you can push through and complete that manuscript.

You've completed your manuscript! Now what? The fourth floor is about going public with your work. When you're at this stage of writing, there are a lot of decisions to make. Do you pursue traditional publishing or indie publishing? What kinds of marketing should you be doing now, even if you don't have a book out? What if you fail at it? Or worse, what if you succeed?

One crucial component of writing success is frequently forgotten about or dismissed. I'm making that our Rooftop Garden. That is the step of celebrating our accomplishments. Celebrating each step towards completing the manuscript. Celebrating sending it out. And celebrating getting back to work on a new one.

This isn't a big book. I don't believe writers should spend all their time on writing books. They should be writing. Use this book as you need. Perhaps you've already got your foundation and you're getting to work and putting the words on the page but you're stuck at the murky middle. Feel free to skip to that part.

This may not be a big book but I am going to ask you to make some significant changes to the way you view writing, your time, and yourself. For this book to be it's most effective at helping you find writing success, it is important that you take the time to do the journaling and the worksheets. Don't expect to complete everything in one sitting. Take your time. Do it over several days or several weeks. In the meantime, write! Because writing success is all about getting the words down on the page.

THE FOUNDATION

SETTING THE FOUNDATION

Allow me to talk architecture for a bit. When designing a building, the foundation of that building is the first to be developed. Without a foundation, there is nothing for the rest of the project to be built upon. Architects and engineers consider the longevity of the building, how tall and wide the building will be, the weight of the structure, and the sturdiness or vulnerability of the ground beneath the building, calculating all factors into the design of the foundation.

When a building has a weak foundation, that building is prone to sinking, crumbling or washing away. The Leaning Tower of Pisa is the perfect example of a building with a weak foundation. It's a great tourist attraction, but it is pretty much useless for any other purpose, certainly for the purpose it was built for.

On the other hand, a building with a strong foundation can withstand earthquakes such as the TransAmerica Building in San Francisco, or break-ins, like that of Fort Knox.

Let's compare the three.

The Leaning Tower of Pisa is 1833 feet tall. It was built on a 3 meter foundation set in weak, unstable subsoil, causing the structure to sink on one side. Thankfully, construction of the tower had ceased for nearly a century, so by the time the upper half of the tower was added, the soil had had time to settle. Had the soil not had time to settle, the entire building would have toppled. There have been several efforts to stabilize the tower, the last one being in 2008.

This has been done by removing the soil from the upper side of the foundation.

Let's compare that to the TransAmerica Pyramid in San Francisco. It's foundation is also 3 meters thick, but it is made of concrete, on stable soil, to fit a floor area of 49,000 square meters. The TransAmerica Pyramid was built to withstand earthquakes, with the full weight of 300 miles of steel rebar, 12,000 cubic meters of concrete, and 260 meter height taken into account.

Fort Knox, on the other hand, that is, the United States Bullion Depository at Fort Knox—you know, where the Unites States government keeps their gold—has need of a different kind of foundation. It isn't built to support a tall building, it is built to withstand break-ins. The foundation is lined with granite walls, has a twenty-one inch thick blast-proof door. The vault casing is twenty-five inches thick.

I don't know about you, but I would rather have the solid foundation of Fort Knox beneath me, than the unstable foundation of the Leaning Tower of Pisa. To have a solid foundation allows you to build a sold writing career without worrying that it, and you, will crumble and fall apart at any moment.

That doesn't mean the foundation can be ignored once it's been built. It does still need to be maintained. Time can age it. The atmosphere and our goals change. And sometimes parts of it need to be shifted or replaced. That is perfectly OK.

We don't just have the *right* to have a strong foundation, we *must* make it strong, in order to succeed.

What follows are elements necessary for a strong foundation.

No Guarantees

One of the most important, but also the hardest principles for writers to accept, is that there are no guarantees that what you write will sell. It may well sell on your first or one-hundredth submission. But it also means it might not sell even when you have a top New York agent sending it out.

So why am I including this as a part of building a solid foundation? This isn't an effort to discourage anyone; rather, I want it to be a freeing concept.

Think about it for a moment. How stressful is it to sit down to write something new, when you're thinking about what is selling right now? It's all in the genre and the kind of story you don't like to write. Every time you start to write something new, you question it. You think it is terrible and it doesn't match what is out there so you scrap it and start over.

I get it. We are trying to write something that will sell to provide us income, success, to make it all worthwhile. If we aren't submitting it with the plan of getting it published, writing would truly be a hobby, something to do when we had nothing else to do. We'd still write, it's what we do, it is at the very core of our being, but we wouldn't be putting in the time or effort.

But writing to what is trending now doesn't work. What is hot now, may not be hot in a year or two when your book is done and making the submission rounds.

The market is out of your control.

Without worrying about whether it is commercial, marketable, or literary enough, you are free to write the story you want to write.

When you write without such worry, you are more likely to write a better story, and you might surprise yourself with your creativity and the imaginative story you produce.

This isn't to say that the saleability of a story should never be considered. It absolutely should be, just not as part of the foundation of a writing career. Worrying about the business end of writing is at best makes for a saggy or fractured foundation that threatens your writing career as soon as, and every time a rejection comes back.

You cannot control the market. You *can* control your storytelling and writing time.

Put the business end of writing aside until the end of the writing project. Before you write, think about the theme of the story, what you are trying to say with it. Think about the appeal of the characters. Make sure it's a good story, in whatever genre or style you want to write. As you polish it and start preparing to submit it, that's when you determine what category, what genre it fits into, and to whom to send it.

Know Why You Write

If you have ever taken a writing workshop, chances are you've been asked this question: Why do you write?

As a Writing Success Coach, it's one of the first questions I ask potential clients. Why do you write?

Some people believe there should only be one correct answer. I'm not one of those people. I believe there are many reasons someone chooses to write. I also believe that those reasons can change depending on the project and even the time of day.

There are multiple components to the question about why someone writes. They want to know what inspires you to write. They want to know what you love about writing. Is it the process, the world you're creating, the characters? Is it telling stories that you love? And then there are the practical reasons someone writes like the dream of seeing their stories in print in the bookstore, or proving to people who said you can't write, that you can.

I don't know of a single answer to "Why do you write?" that sums up all of the components nicely, do you?

As you contemplate the big question about why you write, think about what it is that keeps you coming back to writing, to sitting down and putting the words on the page.

I often think about quitting writing. It's natural. This is a tough business. Then the thought of giving up on my dream breaks my heart more than any rejection could. I also think about what would be expected of me if I wasn't writing. It terrifies me.

There is a lot said about the sacrifices we make to pursue writing. Sacrificing time with friends and family, going out several nights a week. I talk about them in greater depth a little later in this book. For me, they were never sacrifices. I'm too much of an introvert. But even so, I would rather spend time writing than socializing. Writing used to be that way for you. It was something you would rather do than spend your time on anything else. What was it about writing that drew you to it so powerfully that it was the only thing you wanted to do?

Knowing what your reasons are for writing, will support you when your writing life and career are questioned or shaken.

Perhaps your reasons are existential. Writing is who you are. Writing is life. Being a writer is all you have ever wanted to be.

Perhaps your reasons focus on your ambitions. You love the challenge of learning the craft, creating the perfect sentence, and experimenting with characters and story. You want to see your name on the New York Times Bestsellers list. You want your stories to be read and made into top grossing movies and TV shows. You want to give readings at schools. You want to inspire young people to read. You want your stories to influence the way your readers view the world. You want someone who has read your work, to connect with the characters and to tell you that your work helped them through a difficult time.

Perhaps your reasons are more basic. You love living in and creating imaginary worlds. You want to prove to childhood classmates, teachers, or anyone else who said you couldn't do it, that you have succeeded.

Perhaps your reasons are far more fundamental and at the core of your beliefs. You have something to say and you know that others will want to read it. Writing helps you understand the world around you. Writing helps you understand your history, and yourself.

Maybe all of these are your reasons, and more.

The more reasons you have for writing, at all levels, gives you more to fall back on, when things get tough. If one reason gets taken away, you have many more to hold you up.

Think about your reasons for writing, write them down, and keep them somewhere you can access them when you need them.

Why do you write?

Why are you Writing This Story?

This is one of the aspects of the foundation which is the most project specific and will likely always need renovation. Nevertheless, it is a crucial aspect of succeeding as a writer and will help keep you going.

Before you begin each writing project, ask yourself why you want to write that story. Why is it important that you write that particular story? Is it the theme, the characters, the mix of genres, the adventure told in a new way? What do you hope to learn from writing it? Are you going to research a new scientific theory or learn some of the history of a country? Are you going to learn that you can finish a novel in a year or a short story in a week? What areas of your writing skill will you develop by writing this story? Are you going to work on your plot development, inner conflict, description?

As New York Times Bestselling author, David Morrell, best known as the author of First Blood, said at the talk he gave at World Fantasy in Calgary, 2008, to spend a year on a novel is a lot of your time. What makes this writing project worth your time, and energy? Why are you willing to give up time you could be spending with family and friends, on this project?

When we have strong reasons for writing a story, we are less likely to be distracted by that shiny new story idea that inevitably pops up during those long, isolated hours of writing. Dropping one project for the shiny new project seems like a great idea, and then half-way through and it is no longer a shiny new project, and another shiny new project pops up. Far too often this leads to a trail of incomplete stories. Incomplete stories do not equal success.

Once again, the more reasons you have for writing each story, the stronger your foundation. Give it enough time, you may also quiet naturally discover what your brand or theme as an author is: what makes a story by you, a story by you. You'll find patterns in subject matter, or types of plot lines or characters you like to write about, regardless of genre or format.

For each writing project, write down your reasons for writing that story. What do you hope to personally gain from this story? Is it that you're passionate about the subject? You want to understand this issue on the perspective of a character who comes from a very different background than you. You want to explore a different culture or understand your own better. Maybe you want to try a different style or genre. Or maybe you love the genre, the world and characters you're writing about. Maybe you want to see if you can go from the first words to final product in a year or six months.

Now write down what you want to gain professionally from writing this story. Are you looking to explore a new genre or subgenre? Are you attempting a new style of writing? Are you trying to finish a manuscript in a certain amount of time? Are you planning to send this manuscript to agents? Is this story going to exercise your descriptive abilities? Or maybe you'll be working on character conflict or dialogue.

Place and Space

Most writers dream of having the perfect writing office, a place we can retreat to every day, a place that has all the things we love and the right atmosphere for writing. There have been more than a few blog posts and newspaper articles featuring writers, and their writing spaces.

My ideal office would be in a cabin somewhere along an ocean coast, so I can listen to the waves all day. There would be a bay window with a super-cozy window seat where I could read and listen to the waves. The walls would all be built-in bookshelves.

I don't live anywhere near the ocean, I live in the Canadian Prairies in an apartment. The closest I get to the ocean is living along the Red River. It's not the same. But just because I can't have my ideal writing place, doesn't excuse me from writing.

I like to write in my living room, but I'm not always at home. If I want to write, I have to be able to write in all kinds of places and situations.

Prolific writers, and writers facing deadlines, write anywhere and everywhere. Standing in line at the grocery store, waiting at the airport, on the plane, in cars (not while driving unless they're dictating), while going for hikes, and of course while sitting in coffee shops.

You see, while having an ideal office space, or even simply a home base in which to write, is great and helps us get into the mindset that when we're in that space, we write, we can't always be in that place. Being able to write in multiple locations means that if something happens to the home base, you can still write. If you're travelling and on a tight deadline, you can still write.

A strong foundation isn't having an ideal writing place, it is being able to write in less than ideal places.

For many years I was a closet writer. I wrote at night when everyone else was sleeping. I wrote between classes at University. I wrote anytime I had a few minutes and no one I knew was around. I used to write on the bus going to work. It wasn't ideal, but it was what I was able to do. What it prepared me for, was the ability to write most places when I have a few minutes. It also prepared me for handling ambient noise and ignoring noises that might otherwise distract others. This helps me a lot when I go to writing retreats when there are anywhere from three to thirty writers in a room clacking away at their computers. It means I can pick up and go to retreats and not worry about getting into the story because I have the flexibility. What it didn't prepare me for, was writing in silence. I'm terrible with it. I need ambient music on, or the television going in the background. Sports are best for that because I don't really have to pay attention.

I want you to have that flexibility. Train yourself to write anywhere and at any time. Break free from only writing when the kids are sleeping or at school. Break free from only writing in your office. Once the contract comes, you have deadlines. When that happens, you can't take two years to write your next book.

I'll talk specifically about scheduling time to write a little later, especially for those of you with a day job, but it is also important to be able to squeeze in writing time whenever you can. Learn to write in the car while waiting to pick up the kids from their activities. Write on your lunch break at work. Write if you have some down time at work, instead of going on Facebook or Pinterest. The more places you are able to write, the more places you will write. You will find the time to write. The more you write, the stronger the story will be in your mind and you won't have to take time to think about where you were going with it.

Treat writing as a career now. If you do, you will be more productive and you will be better prepared when the contract and editor-imposed deadlines come.

Setting a Routine

Writing in multiple locations can be difficult. It is a challenge switching focus and moving into creative thinking and into the story. But it isn't impossible.

I love watching sports. I've become particularly fond of watching the athletes for the routines they have developed to help them perform, to reset their minds for the task at hand. Broadcasters call these routines superstitions, but they are, in fact, psychological behaviour modification. If you perform well after having a steak dinner and listening to *Iron Man* by Black Sabbath, and you do these two things before a couple of games, the brain connects them with doing your best.

The best athletes also have their in-game routines that help them focus between points. It's called re-setting, to eliminate all distractions and negative thoughts, to perform at their best. In hockey, goaltenders do it after they are scored against *and* after making a big save. Curlers do it when preparing to throw the rock. Tennis players do it between every point. Track athletes do it before they run. The re-setting routine can be something as small as tapping the stick against each goal post, or flipping hair off the shoulder, wiping the rock, then brushing your hands on your knees. Tennis player Maria Sharapova jogs to the wall behind her, fixes the strings on her racket, jogs in place a few times, then returns to the baseline. Rafael Nadal's routine is far more extensive and includes wiping his forehead, wiping the tip of his nose, tucking his hair behind his ears, and giving his shorts a tug, among other things.

As odd as these behaviours are to the casual observer, these re-setting routines have helped make them the top athletes in the world.

We don't have to be athletes to have this kind of brain connection between setting, action, and performance. It is very much a matter of Pavlov's dog, which was trained through positive reinforcement to salivate whenever he heard a bell. Or, if you'd prefer, we can call it neuroplasticity: the re-training of the neural paths in the brain through linking certain actions with performance.

How does this help us as writers? If you set yourself a small routine, before you write, your brain will associate that behaviour with writing. You find it easiest to write in your favourite armchair at home, but armchairs aren't portable. Is there anything you do at home that helps put you into writer mode? Perhaps it's a cup of coffee out of your "Just Write" mug, using a specific pen, or using a specific program on your computer. Maybe it is taking a minute to write down your to-do list and whatever is bothering you and setting it aside until after your writing session.

I bought a new laptop last year and decided it was to be only for writing. While I'd never done anything truly intentional—other than not downloading any games on it—the fact that it was a conscious decision has kept it that way. I may be on the laptop writing and when I need to check my e-mail or look up something online, I take out my phone instead of switching to a browser on my computer, even though that would be the easier thing to do.

What is your current pre-writing routine? How can you make it portable? What will work in line at a grocery store, at a coffee shop or lunchroom, and at a writing retreat?

The shorter and more portable the routine you set yourself, the easier it will be to focus on the writing ahead of you. You'll be able to write in many locations and circumstances. This builds your foundation in a couple of ways.

The first is that like having multiple reasons for writing, the more locations you can write in, the more you will be able to do. And should something happen to one place—by which I mean the kids are driving you crazy and you need to get out of the house for a while, or there's a party, or your allergies are acting up and you need to get out, or you're on vacation or traveling to a conference—you have others you can turn to.

It will also provide you a foundation of greater productivity. Your writing time will no longer be limited to a specific time and place and you will be able to get yourself into the right frame of mind to make better use of your time.

Remember: When you write regularly, daily, and think about your story's plot issues even when you're not writing, you're keeping your story at the forefront of your thoughts. When that happens, you are mulling over ideas even when you're not writing, and you will be more eager to get back to the writing, wherever you are.

Keep Your Eyes on the Prize

On his 1991 album *Brainstorm*, Young M.C. rapped about "Keeping your eyes on the prize." To go for what you want, to not lose focus, even when circumstances seem to be against you or knocking you down, and keep your eyes on the prize.

When we are focused on what we want, we will do what we need to do to get there. We will look for alternate paths when the road we're on turns out to be a dead-end.

Athletes determined to make it to, and win, the Olympics, don't let anything get in their way even when they're sidelined for a while by injury.

Being a writer and pursuing publication, I think, has more opportunity for abstract set-backs. I think I like sports so much because I'm envious. Their results are entirely measurable. They know if they run in a certain time or execute plays or maneuvers the way they're supposed to, they'll win. Writing, on the other hand, is entirely subjective. What one editor thinks is complete garbage, another might love. What I think is terrible writing, someone else might think it is amazing, a perfectly written book. That means we might have to find alternative routes to what we want, such as starting out with short stories, or self-publishing. It also means we have to work harder to not be distracted by the plethora of alternatives.

Keep your eyes on the prize.

What is the end result you're after? Is it to be a bestseller on international book tour? Do you want to win the Pulitzer or Booker award? Is it to have movies and television shows made of your work? Is it to have several books lining the shelves of bookstores, with an end-cap display? Is it to be published by a specific publishing house?

The only constant in the ever-fluctuating industry of publishing, is writing.

You cannot achieve any of your ultimate authority goals without putting the words on the page. Beyond that, it is up to you how you pursue your ultimate goal. Some writers find success after publishing short stories for a few years. There are those who have posted a few chapters on their blog and were signed. Wattpad and other self-publishing avenues are also viable options.

What do you want? What do you need to do to get there? What will you do to get it?

Once you know what the end goal, the prize, is, you can break down all the things you need to do to get there. Breaking it down into smaller steps, more realistic, attainable gaols, will make the ultimate goal feel possible. When dreams are possible, we try harder to achieve them.

A lot of the side roads and publishing alternatives, can throw a lot of distractions at us. At first we'll see them as networking opportunities, or a vital aspect to building our platform, and online presence. Writing guilds or collectives are great for networking and finding support among writers, but also ask for a lot of volunteer time. Self-publishing is a great way to keep creative control and get your work out faster, but it takes a lot of time to format the book right and get all the details done, and money to hire someone to edit, do cover art, and perhaps do the formatting for you. Short stories are a great way to get your name noticed, but even though they're called "short" they take a lot of time and effort to write, which can get in the way of writing larger projects.

Writer's organizations and conferences are amazing for networking, resources for improving as a writer, and that oh-so important support system. They need a lot of volunteer hours which eats into your writing time, but you never know what industry professionals you might meet.

With each option and opportunity, weigh its value against that of your ultimate and immediate goals. Is there enough value in it? Are there enough networking opportunities? Is this really what you need to do to get to the next step toward your ultimate goal? Or will it take up hours of your time, sap your energy, and keep you from writing?

When you know what your ultimate goal is, you are better able to keep your focus on it, strengthening your position, your foundation, as a writer.

Furthermore, when you break down those smaller goals, you strengthen your foundation of resolve and you build it up with smaller successes, which in turn proves you can accomplish your goals.

Keep your smaller goals realistic and within your control. You can't control making the Bestsellers list or winning an award. You can't control what an agent or editor thinks of your work. You can control how often you write and how many words you get on the page when you sit down to write. You can control your growth and development as a writer. Take classes, read books, receive feedback on your work. All of these contribute to your development. You can control your submitting process: choosing the markets to submit to, and how often you send out your work.

Give yourself lots of time to reach your ultimate goal. Don't expect to have a publishing contract in six months if you haven't written a word yet. Write a certain number of words a day, or write for a certain amount of time. I'll talk more about setting achievable and exceedable goals in the section on Getting to Work.

Know what steps you need to get to where you want to go. If there is a step you don't know how it works or how to get there, research it. The publishing industry isn't a secret society. There are resources online and in your city, that will help you figure out what you need to do.

Make sure that your smaller goals are focused on getting you to that ultimate goal. You may want to create a vision board with your ultimate goal on it and keep it near your primary (but not only) writing space. You may want to write down what your daily word goals are and keep them where you can see them as well. Ask yourself each day what you will do today toward your goal. When you find yourself distracted by games or TV, ask yourself if doing these activities will help you achieve your goals.

Support System

Writing can be difficult. It can be isolating and it feels like every rejection is a personal attack. It can make years of slogging, of taking classes, getting feedback, and developing our skills in the craft feel like it was all for nothing. When those rejections come, they hit us like tiny daggers into the heart. Then some young prodigy gets a major book deal with their first draft, on their first submission, and we wonder why we bother.

To survive in this industry, to stand strong when the earthquakes of rejection threaten to destroy us, we need to have a strong support system. It is the support of family and friends that holds our foundation together.

Surround yourself with people who will cheer for you when you get the book contract and sit in the front row at your book launch, and also be there for you when the rejections come in. Who is going to give you honest and constructive feedback on your writing? Who will take care of the dishes and the kids so you can have a few extra minutes for writing when that deadline looms?

Family and friends may be proud of you for pursuing your dreams, but they may not be as supportive as you need them to be if they continually interrupt you or invite you out during your writing time. Their acts of sabotage are often subconscious or unintentional at best, but they are acts of sabotage nonetheless, and they will chip away and erode your foundation.

Boundaries with family and friends are necessary, and we'll talk about that a little later. Often their sabotage comes from them not understanding the importance of writing in your life. They don't understand why you would open yourself up to so much potential rejection, or what the purpose is for spending so much time sitting alone, writing stories.

Let your family and friends in on the process. Help them understand why writing is so important to you, and show them how much work it is.

Let them see the pages you have written over the last few weeks or months. Show them your editing process. Share with them the kinds of critiques you give and receive. Share with them the details of the publishing industry. So many people think you write and your book comes out instantly. Tell them how long you have been submitting your book, how long it takes to hear back from agents. Tell them what the normal advance is for a first-time author in your genre. They will likely question why you spend so much time on your writing, especially knowing what you know about the industry. But they will also be extra proud of you when you *do* finish your book and get it out on submission.

One of the best side effects of getting my M.A. In Writing Popular Fiction, was that my family finally understood and respected my writing time. They didn't get it before. They told me that I would never make money at it, I should keep it a hobby. Intentionally or not, they made me feel like I was wasting my time. Writing a novel for grad school was great. They saw it as homework for a higher degree. That alone gained a lot more respect from them. But that couldn't last forever. It was when my parents came for my graduation, which included my thesis defense where I read from my novel and answered questions. They saw the results that could be achieved from the work I had put in, how serious I was, and really, they saw me in my world, where I belonged. That was when things changed. I let them in and it forever changed things. I now have their unconditional support.

Who supports you? Are you part of a writers group or other writing organization? If not, where can you find that support? What can you do to show your family how important writing is to you?

Ask them for their support, even if they don't understand why you choose this life. Ask them to support you because they love you. Let them know that you will be more likely to succeed with their support.

FIRST FLOOR: DREAMING BIG

DREAMING BIG

We have taken our time and built a solid foundation to support our writing life. Now it is time to start building that writing life. It is here, on the first floor, during the early stages of each writing project, or in the early days of pursuing writing, that we have the freedom to dream big. At this stage, anything is possible. It is an exciting time, but it can also be scary to take those first steps, put those first words down, take our dreams and make them a reality.

What we put into place here is what shapes the future of our writing project and our writing careers. Because what is designed now affects the rest of the building, take time to develop what you want it to look like. Unlike home renovations or actual buildings, though, we are not limited by budget. Our supplies are the skills we develop. We can make our plans as grand as we want. They may take more time to come to fruition, but that is all right because we have the time. We're not limited. This is your opportunity to put into the plan anything you want.

In a lot of ways, this first floor is where we get to be most creative. What do you want your writing career to look like? What kind of book or story do you want to write? What is the theme of your book? How elaborate and complicated do you want the plot to be? How many characters do you want in the story? What are their personalities like? They can be anything you want them to be.

Too often we limit ourselves and our thinking. As we've grown into adulthood, we've learned to dream small, if at all. We're faced with bills and work and family, which limit our activities giving us only a little freedom for change. If we don't see something as an immediate and practical option, we dismiss it.

We're writers. We don't have to live by that rule. This is our chance to reach for the stars. This is the part where we set aside the publishing industry, publishing trends, and genre categories, to write what we want to write. You can be as grandiose as you want. No one has to see this part!

Free Your Mind

As great as it is to have the freedom to dream, it isn't always easy to do. It takes time and practice to break out of our immediate and utilitarian thinking. I bet if I were to ask you right now what you wanted your writing career to be, you would give me one of two responses: 1) I'd like to sell a story or get a book contract; or 2) I'm going to be bigger than Stephen King and J.K. Rowling combined, ha, just kidding, just want to sell a book.

Am I right? Selling a story or getting a book contract is amazing. Is that it then? After the one story or book, are you done writing? Or is that sale a giant first step in a writing life? If you want to be bigger than Stephen King and J.K. Rowling combined, don't laugh it off. You'll have to work extra hard for it, and you may not get there, but why not try for it?

What about the story you want to write? You might be thinking that you'd like to write something with robots and dinosaurs set in the Middle Ages, but Zombies are still pretty hot so you should write something like that.

If you're passionate about a Medieval Robot Dinosaur book, write it! You can't control if it will be picked up by a major publisher, but you can't control that with a zombie book either, so why not write something you love?

For your writing career, ask yourself: What do I want? Is that enough? If not, what do I really want? Not tomorrow, but five, ten, or maybe twenty years from now. What do I want my writing life to look like?

The bills, the job, the family, they can all be worked into the end goal. Look past them. Close your eyes, take a deep breath, relax.

What about the story you want to write? Forget publishing trends. Don't try to guess what the editors of a themed anthology are looking for. What is the story you want to tell? Is that really what you're passionate about? When you decided to submit to that anthology, what was the first idea to pop into your head? What was it that connects with you, that made you think "I could submit something for that?" For your novel or other short stories, think about why you write, what you're passionate about, what you have to say to your readers.

Freeing your mind means getting really honest with yourself. It is best to do this when you have a bit of alone time, or are out for a walk and you have time to think. It is all right to stare out the window or at nothing at all, and let these questions percolate. Go for a walk or some other exercise which will distract your Inner Saboteur and free your subconscious to mull over your story and what you really want to write. You may want to discuss your concerns and ideas with other writers for their input, as long as they focus on the possibilities, and making sure that you are getting at what you want, not imposing their own wishes on you.

In whatever way you do this, be honest with yourself. No one has to see what you write, what your brainstorming process and your dreams are, unless you want them too.

WHAT'S STOPPING YOU?

It seems important to take a bit of time now to talk about what's getting in the way of your dreams before moving onto taking your ideas from the clouds and putting them on the page. As you've been reading this section, and maybe even starting to dream, you've been thinking, "But what about ..." or "I can't do that." Or, "What if ..."

There are several of those objections that pop up at this point. I call them objections or resistance for a reason. Our bodies tell us when something is physically wrong. We hurt, we get sick. We do the same thing mentally. When we experience change, we get anxious. When we are about to do something risky, we feel fear. The same thing happens when we push ourselves with our writing. It is something different. We are setting ourselves up for rejection, for potential pain. We are trying to protect ourselves.

These objections create doubt in our ability to write, doubt in our writing, and worst of all, they create doubt in ourselves. These objections include fear of failure, fear of not being good enough, fear of rejection, fear of not being original, and fearing that no one wants to read what you write and therefore no one will buy it.

While I generally attribute all of these objections to our Inner Saboteur pretending to protect us, there are underlying reasons behind each one. The ways in which each reason affects us is how the Saboteur chooses which objection to use, and when to use it.

Let's look at each of these objections, each of these fears, find out what they are really about, and how to move past them.

Fear of Failure

The fear of failure isn't just a stand-alone fear. In this case, it also plays a part in all the objections at this stage. I'm breaking it out here and talking about it first because it is so prevalent, but also because it can stand out from the others.

Unfortunately, at times, fearing failure is what prevents us from even getting started on something. Often this fear comes out of past experience such as incomplete projects, you have tried and failed before, or you have received several rejections from the same market. Perhaps projects have been started in the past but never completed. These don't have to be writing projects, but they may definitely include them. Our Inner Saboteur reminds us, all too gleefully, that because we haven't completed anything in the past, we shouldn't waste our time now. Clearly we aren't going to complete this one so we shouldn't bother getting started on another one.

Those other projects don't matter now. You stopped working on them for any number of reasons. What were those reasons? What was your skill level then? Were you passionate about it? Did you have the knowledge you needed, or access to it? No. You didn't have the skills you have now. You didn't have the knowledge you have now. You didn't have the passion, the desire, the interest, you have now. More importantly, you didn't have the foundation you have now. Think about what makes this project different from the others. What makes you different from when you worked on those other projects?

Simply by thinking about the possibility of not completing your project and worrying that it might happen, puts you in a better position than you have been. But you don't want to just stop there. Set yourself measurable goals and challenges to ensure that you do complete it. Give yourself word count minimums you have to reach each day or week, and give yourself a reasonable deadline for each draft. Find yourself an accountability buddy—either a fellow writer or your critique group—to hold you accountable. When you and your accountability buddy reach your goals, reward each other. If you find yourself or your partner falling behind, check in with each other and help each other get back on track with encouragement.

And then there are our past failures. Again, these are not necessarily writing related. Our Inner Saboteur tells us that we've tried to think out of the box before, we've tried to dream big and it got us nowhere in the past, there's no point in trying it again.

Here's the beautiful thing about dreaming big, or thinking outside the box; some of the ideas work and some of them don't, and that's all right. Not every idea we have is going to be perfect. Not every idea we have is terrible. We're not going to know if we have a good idea or not, until we allow ourselves to think them up without restriction. Maybe they'll need to be tweaked, maybe they'll need to be scrapped all together, or maybe, just maybe, they'll be golden. You won't know which one it is, until you give it some time to breathe and grow and blossom. No one has to see our ideas, our dreams. You can write them down and tuck away the ones you won't use right away. Some day you may come back to them and they'll be perfect. Allow yourself that time and space to dream without restriction, without worry, because you won't know if it is what you're looking for, until you try it.

Our Saboteur isn't satisfied with reminders of our past failures. He then makes us think about the consequences of our failure—what we will have lost—so it is better to not start at all. We start to think about all the time we're going to spend on the project, and even though we have solid reasons for wanting to write it and we can say that those reasons will make it all worthwhile even if it doesn't sell, we doubt if that's really true. The point of pursuing a writing career is publication, right? So if it doesn't sell, isn't that failure? And all that time will have been spent away from family and friends with nothing to show for it. Sure, we may have learned something about the craft of writing, and enjoyed the research, but that doesn't help anyone but ourselves.

Success is getting the words on the page, polishing them up, and sending them out. We cannot control what editors and agents think, and we cannot control what the market dictates. Selling to one of the big publishers isn't your only option any more. There are smaller presses, smaller magazine and e-zine markets with great reputations that may be a better fit. Self-publishing is also a viable option thanks to e-books and Print on Demand services reducing costs. But you can't expect grand returns the moment you finish your story. As much as we all wish editors and agents could see our genius while we're writing, and offer us a contract before the story is complete, that's not how it works. You have to complete your story, polish it, send it out, and then wait. You may have to send it out to several markets. And while you're waiting for responses to come back, you're taking what you've learned on that first story, and applying it to the next one you're starting to write, which will be bigger and better than the last. The only thing that is a wasting your time, is not writing.

So what is really behind this fear? It's about personal loss, leaving our comfort zone and daring to dream. We won't lose time with our family and friends if we don't write. We won't have spent hours on our own when we could have been watching all the TV shows our friends were talking about and then we would have been able to be a part of their conversations. We would have been following everyone's activities on Social Media and been far more socially savvy. We wouldn't be putting ourselves at risk of rejection. We would be safe, doing the same things we always do, the same things that everyone expects of us.

Rather than thinking of stepping out of your comfort zone as something bad, rather than thinking of rejection as bad, rather than thinking about what you have to lose, think about what you have to gain from taking these risks. Think about all that you will learn and how much you will grow. Embrace the fear. Let it motivate you to do more, be a better writer, be more focused in your use of your writing time so it isn't a waste.

Fear of Not Being Good Enough

When we fear not being good enough, we are doubting our skills and abilities as writers. We are basing this fear on our past output, and comparing ourselves and our work to the works of all the great writers who have gone before us and grace the shelves of our bookstores.

When we're starting out, we are at a disadvantage. We don't have the same skills and abilities of writers who are already published, and yet if we want to break in, we need to have them.

If you're at the point where you've decided to take your writing seriously enough to start submitting it, you've already developed many of the skills necessary. The problem is that we don't realize how much we've improved. We're still seeing our writing as those early drafts we wrote when we first put the proverbial pen to paper. Every now and then it is worth taking a look back at our earlier writing projects to see how far we've come. Of course, you have nothing to compare those past projects to if you haven't written anything new.

That's not the only way to know that you are improving. Make a list of all the writing classes you've taken, or writing books you've read and learned from. Remember all the books you've read, some by your favourite authors, books you've loved, and others you've hated. From each one you have learned something about the writing craft. Think about what you knew about writing when you first decided you wanted to write a story, any story. How much more do you know now?

Remember that your style of writing isn't going to be the same as anyone else's. There may be some comparisons, but you don't want to be the same as someone else. We are all individuals. We all see the world differently. We all tell stories differently.

Does that mean you're now "good enough?" Good enough is a subjective state. There are so many factors that play into whether your story sells, and most of them depend on what the editor is looking for, the market at the moment, and what their marketing department decides—all of which are out of your control. Good enough also suggests a desire to stop growing. Continued growth as a writer is critical to success now and in the future. Other writers around you will continue to develop their craft and surpass you if you don't continue to do the same.

Are you good enough? You are good enough for now, with all the knowledge you have now. Maybe that story will sell, maybe it won't. You have done enough to demonstrate your skill and knowledge that you have at the moment. As you grow as a writer, you will look back on what you've written today and will see things you would change. But again, you're not going to get to that point, if you don't start something now.

Are you good enough? You won't know until you have put the words on the page and polished them.

Fear of Rejection

The fear of rejection. We all have it. It's why asking someone out on a date is so filled with angst. No one likes to be told "no." We take it personally. That it is us they are saying no to, and not our work. That may be the case for being turned down for a potential date, but it is not the case for our writing.

Some of the reasons for a rejection: the story truly isn't the kind of story they are looking for right now; the story wasn't told compellingly to catch their attention; it doesn't quite fit the kinds of stories they publish; they just bought a similar story; it doesn't meet their guidelines; a particular editor doesn't like the story (but another one might). The only one of these reasons remotely in your control is telling the story in a compelling manner, and even that is a subjective opinion.

So how do you get past this fear?

Until you have written, polished, and submitted something, there is nothing to be rejected. Until you have something written and polished, you don't know what you have—what market it should be sent to, what the theme is, what the story is. Don't reject it before you've written it. If you do, the only one rejecting you, is you, and that's a personal rejection.

It helps too, to realize that rejection is a part of the process of submitting. I would love to tell you that the first rejection you receive is the hardest, but that just isn't true. There are times when you submit to markets that you hope will accept your work and you're disappointed but not really surprised if they reject you. And then there are times when you are submitting to your ideal market and you are devastated if they say no to you. Even if those rejections are "good" rejections, where you receive personal feedback from editors and requests to see more of your work—a definite sign that you are improving—it doesn't take away the pain of not receiving a contract.

The rejections don't get easier, but you can deal with them. When you know how to deal with rejection, you no longer have to fear it. Know that the rejection isn't personal. There are a lot of reasons that go into making publishing decisions. Know that you have options for your work. When that rejection comes, give yourself an hour or a day to grieve, yes grieve, acknowledge the pain, and then send that story out again. While you're waiting for that story to sell, write something else, something new, exciting, different, and better.

Fear of Not Being Original

Originality. I think it is the bane of every writer at one point or another in their careers. Imitation may be the sincerest form of flattery, but in the writing game, it could lead to charges of plagiarism at the worst. At best, you would be labeled "Like (name famous writer here) but not nearly as good." Editors will refuse to publish something because they have recently published something similar and yet it is a compliment to be called "The next (name famous author here)." And editors will sometimes look for books that are similar to what is doing well for them.

Originality can be very difficult to determine in our own work. I remember submitting a story for critique and it wasn't until I was sitting in the workshop that I realized I'd completely ripped off "Lara Croft: Tomb Raider." I didn't get that from the feedback I received; it was my own impression of my work. My feedback was that it was similar in style to something Ursula K. LeGuin wrote; not an imitation, but similar in style. I was pleased with the comparison. The group workshopping my work didn't think it was like "Lara Croft" at all.

What happens is that we become so paranoid about being original, that we start to see other people's work in our own, whether it is there or not. To avoid unnecessary influence, some writers don't read fiction in the same genre as what they are writing, or reading any kind of fiction while working on a first draft.

If you find that works for you, then go for it, but I don't know that that's the answer. I think that writers need to read broadly and always. If you're struggling with one aspect of the craft of writing, you might read something that sparks an answer for you.

I struggled for a long time with my writing. It was OK, but I knew it was missing something. I just couldn't put my finger on what it was that was missing. I've read hundreds of books in my lifetime, so you would have thought I'd be able to spot what I was missing right away, but I couldn't. Not until I chose to read some of the literary masters like H.G. Wells, Robert J. Sawyer, and Marian Keyes, with the purpose of figuring out what they had that I didn't, that I realized I was missing the little subtle touches of description and emotion. Realizing that, I was able to work on it and grow as a writer.

Yes, you need to be vigilant as you're writing. Be aware of any obvious forms of imitation. The best way to keep your work original is to have several beta readers read your work after the first draft is done, after you've had some time to edit and revise it. Your readers, your critique partners, will tell you if there are originality issues you need to address.

Originality of ideas is just as easy an issue to deal with. As you dream and brainstorm your story ideas, you're going to want to throw them aside because "that's been done before." Depending on which expert you listen to, there are only three to seven stories in the world. It's what you do with the story, your own underlying theme that you're applying to it, that makes each story original. You can also use these masters for story ideas. There really are no original stories anymore, but there are original ways of telling them. You can blend genres or tropes, give them a twist. Tell a story from your viewpoint, rather than what every other author has done.

So maybe the bookstores are flooded with vampire novels, but you're really passionate about writing a vampire novel, rather than throwing it out, think about what you are adding to the story to make it unique.

When I attended the Odyssey Writing Workshop, I struggled immensely with coming up with something original. It wasn't until I combined two genres I love: chick-lit with epic fantasy, that I came up with a character and story I loved. That ended up being *Mabel the Lovelorn Dwarf*.

As you dream up those story ideas, before you toss it out, think about what makes the story unique to you.

Fearing No One Will want To Read Your Work

All the other fears have involved doubt in our skill in and knowledge of the craft of writing. Fearing that no one will want to read what we're writing is all about doubting our selves. This is doubting that what we have to say is worth listening to. It's doubting that our opinions are valid. We are doubting that we are worthy of attention and the approval of others.

Moving past this self-doubt isn't easy. It requires deeper self-reflection. It means that rather than depending solely on external sources for approval, we need to look to ourselves for that approval. Again, depending on the kind of person you are, this is easier said than done. But I suspect if you have this kind of fear or objection, you tend to focus on external approval. This is what is called having an "External Frame of Reference". How do you know if this is you?

Think of it this way. If you, in your day job, complete some kind of project or event and it went well, how do you know if you have done a good job, that you've done it right? Do you know, instinctively, that it was amazing and you were perfect at it? Or do you wait for your boss or co-workers to tell you that it was good? What if you think it was great, and your boss isn't happy with it? Does that affect how you think it went?

If it does, if you need to have others confirm your opinions on how an event went or how successful your project went, then you are more of an External Reference kind of person. This isn't always a bad thing. But to be more successful as a writer, there are times, like in the case of fearing that others won't want to read what you write, you need to be a more Internal Reference kind of person.

If you have more of an External Frame of Reference, you lean toward accepting others opinions of what is right or wrong, good or bad. You are strongly swayed by external critiques regardless of how much they may contradict each other, or change your story into one you don't really want to write. You do it because you believe others are better judges than you are, of what is good writing, a marketable story, or appropriate characters. This isn't to say you shouldn't listen to the feedback you receive. You should give it all serious consideration as to whether it makes your story better, the way you want your story to be, or if it changes it. But know what you want. Your name is on the final product. Will you be proud of it?

Until a year ago (at the time of writing), I was almost entirely an External Reference kind of person. While I set my own goals and had my own dreams, I relied on everyone else's opinion for validation. I didn't do a good job at work unless my boss told me I had. I wasn't smart at school until my grades showed me I knew the material. My writing was never any good because I felt like no one said it was.

I'm a female, and growing up, the most common way of complimenting a girl was to tell her she looked nice. I rarely got that compliment, or if I did, I don't remember. It didn't matter if I walked to school believing I looked stylish or with perfect hair, no one ever told me I looked nice. Well, no one but my mom. At school, I was called fat and cross-eyed, and ugly. When no one complimented me, it only confirmed what everyone else was saying. Sure, my mom told me I looked nice, but I didn't believe her. Not just because no one else seemed to agree with her. Too often I'd heard parents talk about how cute their babies are, or how smart their kids were, and always tack on, "Not that I'm biased or anything." My mom *had* to compliment me. She was my mom. Because she had to, it couldn't possibly be true.

When it came to the writing, all those rejections were from people who are supposed to know what is good and marketable. They're in the business. They get paid to know. My critique partners might tell me something is good, but they couldn't possibly really know, they aren't paid to know. How could I, someone typing away in my living room, know?

I say I was this way until just recently, but the seeds of being an Internal Reference person were planted in me several years ago.

I obtained my Master's degree in Writing Popular Fiction from Seton Hill University in January of 2009. At the time of writing, it is still the only MFA program in the United States that focuses solely on genre fiction. I had gone into the program fully expecting to write this serious, epic Fantasy novel that was all political and dark. By that point I'd been working on this novel for a good four or five years and it was in as many iterations, each one becoming more cliche than the previous one because I'd been listening to people who had only critiqued the first few chapters and had all kinds of ideas where they thought the story should go.

I sat down for my first meeting with my mentor, the amazing Anne Harris. I laid out the plan of the novel. She read over my synopsis and essentially said, "There's nothing unique here." Not exactly the response I wanted to hear. Now, I'm a weepy type of person, and I started to cry a little. Anne said, "But we could work at fixing that." My response was, "How long will that take?" I won't lie. It was a disheartening conversation, I'd spent so much time on this novel, it was what I thought I was *supposed* to write, but clearly, from my response, it wasn't a story I wanted to write. Anne asked me how much I cared about the characters. I couldn't answer her. She asked if I cared about them at all. I didn't. I started sobbing at this point. In part, because I was grieving setting aside a book I'd been working on for so long, but mostly because I felt relief that I could set it aside.

So poor Anne is finding tissues for me, thinking she's broken me (her first student). When she gets back, I tell her that I'm relieved. I say, "So here's the other book I want to write, that I was planning on writing when I wasn't working on that other epic monstrosity."

I told her about *Mabel the Lovelorn Dwarf*. She says my face basically lit up when I talked about it. My whole attitude changed. I'd noticed that prior to that meeting, whenever my fellow classmates would ask me what I was writing, I would tell them about the epic monstrosity, but also, and to a greater extent, talk about Mabel. Anne looked at me and said, "It sounds like that's the novel you really want to write, and you feel like you need permission to write it." Right there, she wrote a permission slip in my notebook, to write Mabel. She signed it "A real writer". She was someone in the know.

It was that external permission, that allowed me the freedom to write the book I wanted to write, and to believe in it, to believe that what I had to say was worth writing, that others wanted to read it.

It certainly helped that Seton Hill was such a supportive atmosphere, simply by having the opportunity to immerse myself in a community of like-minded writers for a full week twice a year, with nothing but writing as our focus. I saw my classmates believe in themselves and their stories which helped me believe in myself and my writing. We were all there putting in the work, learning the skills, struggling and growing together. It also helped that my classmates connected with my writing and characters. I started to believe in myself. And yet, I would still say, they were my classmates, they had to be supportive of me, at least to my face. Who knew what they said behind my back?

But the switch didn't truly occur until the summer of 2014. I was going through a rough patch and I was feeling completely overwhelmed with work, coaching and writing. I'd believed in *Mabel the Lovelorn Dwarf* enough to publish it myself, and I was working on a couple of other projects, including the sequel to Mabel. I felt like I was drowning. That I was incapable of doing anything right, or at all. I felt like a complete failure.

I called up a counselor. I bemoaned my existence and my ineptitude. At one point she stopped me and said, "But you have done amazing things. Your actions do not reflect your beliefs about yourself."

I was stunned by the reality being reflected back at me. I'd never been able to look at it objectively before and now I had no choice but to do so. Such a simple concept changed everything for me. It showed me that everything negative I believed about myself and what I had done, because she was completely objective. I didn't know her, she wasn't a friend and she wasn't a relative.

I took time to re-evaluate everything I had relied on others to validate. I looked at all I had accomplished. I had given them all my stamp of approval, had stood behind them, and yet I hadn't believed in them or myself. Now I chose to believe in them, that I had grown, that I had developed the skills, that I knew best when something was or wasn't ready. It was a conscious choice and once I made it, I saw things differently.

That choice changed how I thought about all I'd done. How did that change my need for external approval for my writing? I still need some external approval for it. I wouldn't submit it or publish it if I didn't. I'd leave it in a drawer or on my computer if I only needed my approval. But I realized I could rely on my own judgment. If I thought it was right to publish a book, then it was, even if everyone else thought it wasn't. I learned to rely on my own decisions and beliefs. If I thought I had something worth saying, then I should write it.

No, I can't know if an editor or agent, or even the reading public, will feel the same way. But that is not for me to judge. I can only write what I want to write, and if I'm passionate about it, that passion will come through in the story, which will make it far more compelling than writing something because I think that's what people will want.

I would rather spend time on something I want to write than what I think others want to read. If it doesn't sell, at least I will be happier having spent the time on that project. If I'd spent a year of my life working on something I think people want, and it gets rejected, that would feel like a complete waste of time and would be less satisfying.

When I graduated from Seton Hill, Anne gave me an official permission slip that says, "In perpetuity, Sherry Peters has permission to write whatever she damn well pleases." Signed Anne Harris, a real writer.

I love that permission slip. I have always had it in my living room as a reminder every time I write. But now I take it more seriously. I can write what I want, and if I believe it is worth reading, then I ought to write it. Will there be a financial payoff at the end of it? Not necessarily, but at this stage of writing, that isn't for me to decide.

As one editor said to me, as long as I follow the guidelines and the story fits the genre they publish, it isn't for me to decide if they will accept it or not.

Too often, we self-reject before we're half-way through a story or novel. Because we believe that no one wants to read it, we set it aside and start something new. We do this too early in the writing process. You won't know what you have until you've finished the project. You won't know if anyone wants to read it until you send it out.

If *you* want to read it, then it is worth writing.

We can get past this fear by looking back at our foundation of why we want to write this particular story. Do you care about the characters? The plot? The theme? Your opinions are the only ones that matter right now. What response do you have to your own words? Do they inspire you? Do they connect emotionally with you? Do you identify with, or learn from, the theme?

The market changes. Trends change. Your opinions are the only ones that matter.

Look at everything you have done. What do you think about each of those accomplishments? Do you think you are a failure or a fraud? Do your actions prove it or do they show something different? If they show that you have been successful, how might that then change your thinking about yourself and what you have to say as a writer? If you're having trouble being objective about it, ask a third party to help show you your reality.

To help you with this, I have put together a worksheet which you will find at the end of this book, and a printable version on my website: http://www.sherrypeters.com/blueprintextras. On this worksheet you will write down your accomplishments, next to it, your negative belief about it, and then the objective reality of your success.

We may experience one, all, or none of these fears at any given time. Which fears we experience will change with the project we're working on. It is natural to feel them. Please revisit these tools as you need them. There may be other fears that come up for you. Use the same technique we've used here. Ask yourself what is really behind that fear. What tools do you have to move past that fear? How can you use that fear to your advantage?

THE SATISFACTION EQUATION

The fears we have will probably never go away completely. They may pop up every now and then, in milder forms each time. We've talked about ways to deal with them individually. There also comes a time when you have to ask yourself, what do you really want? Is writing worth facing rejection, and the possibility that no one will buy your work? Is the possibility of getting that acceptance, of selling your work, of writing the story you want to write, worth more than what you might lose by pursuing it? If you were out for dinner with your friends and family, knowing that you are safe, accepted, and a success at work, would you be happy? Or would you sit there still wishing you had taken the chance and written?

Consider Richard Beckhard's Satisfaction Equation, or the Formula for Change:

$D \times V \times FS > RC$

D is the experienced dissatisfaction with the current state/situation,

V is a vision of a desired future state, of what is possible;

FS is the clarity and feasibility of the first steps toward that vision.

The product of all three must be greater than the current resistance to change (RC) for us to take that chance.

In our situation, we'll say that our dissatisfaction is with the status quo, our desire to write, to follow those dreams. To be writing, rather than sitting with family and friends wishing we were writing. The vision, then, is where we see ourselves and our writing in the future, as bestsellers or impacting someone's life in a positive way. The clarity and feasibility will start in the next few pages as we continue to formulate our blueprint. If all of these are greater than the resistance to change, the fears you are encountering, then you can push past, or work in spite of those fears. Then you're ready to set them aside and write. You are ready to not let those fears getting in your way.

If you are at that point, then it is time to free your mind, open it up to those dreams and possibilities of story ideas.

What you want to do is to allow your brain to relax. Set aside your fears about writing, and your daily worries. Rather than being stuck in emotional anxiety, your creativity then has a chance to flow. Everyone has their own way of doing this. I will outline a few suggestions here to get you thinking of ways to nudge forward the creativity. Give them a try. If they work, great. If they don't, maybe something else will work for you.

The first method I'm going to suggest, is called a clearing journal. This is where you take no more than two minutes at the beginning of each writing session, or in this case time allotted for dreaming, to put down all your concerns, all the things you have yet to do that day, whatever is bothering you that might keep you from being relaxed. After the two minutes, you set it all aside. It will be there for you to pick up after your dreaming time is done. What this does is it psychologically relieves you of your worries, if only for a few minutes or a few hours.

Exercising is also a wonderful way to free the creativity in you. Personally, I find walking the most effective. For others it may be jogging or dancing, or any other kind of physical activity, that doesn't require you to think about what you are doing or where you are going. When you are moving, exercising, you're releasing endorphins, that make you feel better, you feel safe, and relaxed. When you're on a familiar path, your body eases into a rhythm which is again relaxing. Your muscles are all working hard, burning energy, distracting the worry part of your brain. You're in your rhythm, you're sweating, your conscious brain can only think left foot, right foot, left foot, right foot. This frees your creative subconscious to work its ideas up into your consciousness. This is a great way to solve plot problems. It's also a great way to see possibilities that you couldn't see before.

One of the things I love about being a writer, is that writers are allowed to sit and stare out the window or at a spot on the carpet for hours, and we're working. Find a seat that's comfortable, or lie in bed, somewhere you are comfortable, relaxed and safe, and allow your mind to wander. This is often what happens to writers when they're about to fall asleep. That's why we always complain about not getting enough sleep because we've come up with our best ideas just when we're about to fall asleep. Having a nice hot shower can also have similar results. I think it's the massaging the scalp that happens when you wash your hair. It massages the thoughts out into the open.

Another suggestion is what New York Times Bestselling author David Morrell refers to as plot talking. This is where you sit down at your computer or with pen and paper, and ask yourself what you really want to write about. Pretend you are a journalist interviewing you. Dig deep. Don't let yourself get away with the easy, off the cuff answers. When you get the story out of you, then interview the story. What does it want to be? Who is in it? What is the conflict? Again, don't go easy on it. Once you have the characters, interview them. Dig for their true motivation. Demand that they be honest with you. Call them out if you catch them lying, if what they're saying doesn't make sense. Write down your question and the answers you receive. It can be fun to come back to if at any point in the story you get stuck, then you have a resource of what you want, a good reminder. You might surprise yourself what you can come up with doing this exercise.

Which leads me to my final suggestion: good, old-fashioned brainstorming. Most people are familiar with brainstorming in the business setting, where everyone in a department is gathered in a room and are asked to shout out suggestions on various topics. Every idea is supposed to be valid, no matter how far-fetched, but inevitably some smarty-pants has something negative to say about all but his or her own ideas. Writer brainstorming is a little bit different. You can do it in a couple of different ways: either by yourself, or with a group of two or three other writers.

If you're brainstorming by yourself, figure out what the problem is, if it's the plot, the characters, theme, story you want to tell, whatever you want to dream big about, and start writing down possibilities. You can make a mind-map, or simply free-write. The only one who can nay-say your ideas is you, so don't. Just let them go. See where they might lead. Maybe you think something is a huge stretch, but you might come back to it in a bit and find that it leads to something else, which leads to another idea, which sparks something in you that screams out that yes, this is the answer.

Brainstorming with a few other writer friends can be a lot of fun. It works really well when all of you have something you want to brainstorm. One person starts with where they're stuck, what they're having trouble with, or what idea they have but need more possibilities. Then the rest of the group thinks on it and comes up with ideas. Again, every idea is valid. Inevitably, something will spark a connection, something you want to explore deeper. Having other people's input gives us other perspectives on our own work and dreams, which we need because sometimes we're simply too close to it to see the bigger picture. It also helps then, to work on ideas for the other members of the group. Not only does it help them, but it might lead to some additional possibilities for yourself.

LUCK FAVOURS THE PREPARED

You've freed your mind, you've pushed aside your fears, and you've dared to dream big. Now what? How do we go about getting those dreams out of the clouds, and make them into a reality? Ask yourself the following: What do you need to do, to make it happen? What needs to change, for it to happen?

Simple questions, with often long and complicated answers.

So let's walk through a couple of examples.

We'll start with the writing career dream first. Where do you see yourself in five, ten, or twenty years as a writer? Let's say you want to be the next J. K. Rowling or Stephen King, with millions of your books being sold, movies and TV series made of your work, and an amusement park based on your work. What can you do to make this happen?

Remember, most of this will be out of your control, but you can put in a lot of work to set yourself up to achieve this dream, or some semblance thereof. Writing is the obvious thing that you have to do, but how much do you need to write? Will it happen through self-publishing or getting published by one of the big publishing houses? What do you need to do to get picked up by one of the big houses? How will you find that agent? What about your writing skills? What more do you need to do to develop them to get to a place where your prose is publishable?

Maybe your dream is to be a self-publishing superstar, one where you make more than a decent living off your writing, and traditional publishing houses are offering you major contracts that you're turning down because you can do it better yourself. What does it take to be that kind of self-published writer? Will you be able to do it with only one book or do you need to produce several books? If you have to produce several books, how often do you have to release them? What about the business end of it, keeping track of sales, taxes, marketing and publicity?

Write down all the things you need to do. If you're not sure about all the steps, do some research. There are writers living those dreams, find out how they did it. You will have to do some things differently simply because of changing times and markets, but the work ethic will be the same.

I'm going to include a word of caution about marketing here. Whether you're traditionally published or self-published, you're going to have to do a lot of the marketing yourself. It's the nature of the changing publishing industry. Feel free to start looking through the material that is available on how to best market yourself and your work, but don't get caught up in it. Everyone seems to be an expert on marketing. Most of what they have to say is the same thing as everyone else, but there are always variations, and each of those variations and tools for marketing are made to seem like they are the answer to your marketing prayers, making you feel like you have to do all of it, and do it now. As I say, feel free to start on it, do some, whatever feels most natural to you, but note that by the time you actually have a book ready to market, the climate will have changed again and things may need to be done differently. The absolute best way to sell your work, is to write the best damn book you possibly can, and write more of them.

Now that you've made a list of all the things you need to do to reach your dream writing career, what, if anything, needs to change in your life, to make it happen? This is probably the scariest question, not to have to answer honestly, but to then implement those changes. What classes do you have available for you to take to develop your craft? What writing books do you need to read, and actually read them, not just buy them and have them sit pretty on your bookcase? What is the time commitment you need to write the amount of words you need to write each day? How will you get it? Will you hire a maid service to free up time from cleaning your house? What about the kids? How will you work around them, or will you ask someone to look after them for you while you're writing? Can you afford to write full time or do you have a day job? If you have a day job, how will you fit your writing around it? Is there a way you can reduce your working hours to make more time for writing? Will you need to change jobs to make that happen? What if that means a reduction in pay? Will you be able to pay the bills and keep food on the table? How will you make yourself and your writing a priority? How will you say no to family and friends so that you can have that time to write?

Now let's talk about your big dream of a novel you want to write. What did you come up with? Is it a Horror, or Science Fiction, or Epic Fantasy series? Maybe it's a literary heart-breaker, or humorous tome.

What do you need to do to make it a reality on the page? How many words will it be approximately? When do you want to have it finished and out the door to editors or to the printers? How many words do you need to write a day to get the first draft done? Do you edit as you write or do you just get all the words down first and edit after? How long will it take you to edit it? Do you have a writing group to critique your work? Do you need to hire an editor? If you're self-publishing, do you need to hire an artist for the cover? How long will each of those things take? Is your end deadline realistic or do you need to extend it a few months? Is it your deadline or your publisher's deadline? If it's your publisher's deadline, how can you make your word counts each day to complete the project on time? What needs to change in your life to make it happen? If it is your own deadline, how will you ensure that you meet it and don't put it off indefinitely?

Write it all down.

Are you feeling overwhelmed with how much you have to do? Take each step and give it a time frame. Give your first draft a time frame such as three months. Give yourself another three or six months for editing. Set out each of your daily writing goals and know that you don't have to write the entire novel in a week, and that you have time, you don't have to do everything at once.

Are you wondering if it will all be worth it in the end?

Ask yourself: what do you really want? Yes, it will take time, and sacrifices will have to be made. Is the dissatisfaction, vision, and clarity, greater than your resistance to change?

What if it is worth it and you decided not to pursue it?

What if you do pursue it and you reach your dreams?

What if you decide not to pursue it, and nothing changes for you?

What do you really want? What are you willing to do to make it happen?

SECOND FLOOR: GETTING TO WORK

GETTING TO WORK

Getting through the dreaming big stage is a, well, a big deal. If it weren't, all those people who suggest stories to writers, or say they wished they could write, or will write when they retire, wouldn't be saying those things, they'd be right here with you, sitting down and writing. Dreaming can be great, and figuring out how to get those dreams on paper can be a lot of fun, but now it is time to actually do the work.

This floor should be simple enough. We have our dreams and how we're going to make them happen. This floor covers the first half of the writing project. It deals with the writing itself, the chosen writing process, prioritization and time management, and building towards a successful finish of the project.

Once again, you will see that several of the supports built into our foundation become necessary to successfully move on to the third floor.

This is the first practical step in taking our dreams from the clouds and making them a reality. On this floor, we're putting the place, space, time, and routine from our foundation into action. We're putting our butt in the chair and writing regularly and consistently, even when we don't feel like it or feel too tired to write.

In this section we're going to talk about figuring out the right writing process for the project we're working on. Are you an outliner or a Pantser? What's the difference? What are the pros and cons of each? We're going to talk about making writing a priority, and ways to set and maintain boundaries with family and friends. We're going to spend some time on something I include in all of my books and workshops, which is setting achievable and exceedable goals. We're also going to look at the obstacles that get in our way at each step, what is behind them, and how we can move past them.

TIME, PRIORITIES, AND GOALS, OH MY!

You didn't think I was going to leave you hanging at the end of Luck Favours the Prepared, did you? I've combined time, priorities, and goals because they are interdependent, and they are crucial for getting yourself into a solid position to finish your writing project. I won't lie, this part is going to be fairly challenging. You will want to resist. You're going to come up with all kinds of excuses why you can't make the changes I'm going to ask you to consider making. We'll get to that resistance in a bit. For now, see this as your opportunity to put yourself and your writing first, to seriously consider how you're going to follow up your big dreams. This is all about making it possible for you to meet your word count targets and deadlines.

To find the time to write, we need to start with making note of what we're doing and when. Take a few days to go through this section. I want you to write down what you do each day and for how long. It doesn't have to be to the minute, but guesstimate as closely as possible. I don't want you to change anything you do this week. I don't want you to leave anything out. This isn't a weight-loss food-diary. I'm not going to judge you for having that chocolate bar. If you do something, whatever takes time, write it down!

What your week might look like:

Monday:
Breakfast – 15 minutes
Get the kids ready for school – 30 minutes (can you tell I don't have any?)
Walk the kids to school – 60 minutes
Work – 3.5 hours
Lunch with co-workers – 1 hour
Work – 3.5 hours
Pick kids up from sitters – 1 hour
Supper – 1 hour
Chauffeuring kids – 2 hours
Cleaning, laundry, and TV time with the hubs. - 3 hours
Sleep – not enough hours!

Do this for each day this week, including the weekend. Keep track of what you're doing. Make note of any patterns you spot.

Remember, for now, I just want you to keep track, don't change anything.

There is a time-log worksheet at the end of the book, and a printable version on my website: http://www.sherrypeters.com/blueprintextras. Print off as many copies as you need.

While you're filling out the time-log, let's move on to having a work/life/writing balance. Is such a thing even possible? I believe it is. I think we need to first define what that balance means. Not everything is going to have equal attention, nor will it always give us equal or super satisfaction. We have to allow that some days will be better than others. And we also have to allow that sometimes, life will get in the way. We have to face the reality that we won't be able to dedicate twelve hours a day to our writing. Therefore, the time we do spend on it will have to be much more focused.

I know, we all want those large chunks of time to focus on our writing, but most of the time, it just isn't realistic. No one wants a day job, but most of us don't earn enough from our writing not to have one. Being a stay-at-home parent has its own challenges to finding writing time as well.

I will also set out this challenge for you to think about: When you do have large chunks of time to spend on your writing, how much of it is actually spent writing, and how much of it is spent checking e-mail and facebook, and maybe tidying a bit around the office, and checking e-mail again, then maybe writing a sentence or two, then getting a snack and checking facebook? You get the point I'm trying to make, right? It isn't always about the amount of time. It's that old saying: Quality v. Quantity.

If you have a day-job, there are a couple of major benefits that I think writers often over-look but should be mentioned as a reminder of why we have them:

Financial Security. I don't know about you, but I've gone without that regular paycheck for over a year, and it was hard. Knowing you have that steady income means you don't have to worry about keeping a roof over your head, food on the table, and your internet connected. That alone frees up a lot of mental and emotional space. It also allows you to enjoy your writing more. I know a few full-time writers, who have high enough advances and film options being continually sold and enough foreign royalties coming in, that they live quite well. But there is constant pressure on them to produce more, and quickly. If they have a bad personal year or two, and there is no book coming out, there is no advance; their income is cut in half. Imagine getting paid five times a year, having to budget that out, not knowing what other money will come in. While I will be more than happy to be that kind of mental and emotional stress because of my writing, I don't want to be there unnecessarily.

Life Experience: I freely admit that I have strong tendencies toward being a hermit. And while great fiction comes out of the imagination, it is truly given life by our experiences. J. R. R. Tolkien said this about writing "The Lord of the Rings": "One writes such a story not out of the leaves of trees still to be observed, nor by means of botany and soil-science; but it grows like a seed in the dark out of the leaf-mould of mind: out of all that has been seen or thought or read, that has long ago been forgotten, descending into the deeps. No doubt there is much selection, as with a gardener: what one throws on one's personal compost-heap."

The leaf-mould is like the drain at the side of the road, where the leaves and twigs collect as the rain-water drains down. It is our life experiences that are the leaves and twigs that gather, both good and bad, that feed our imagination. The people we encounter at work, the antics of our children and neighbours, our tasks, our emotional reactions to all of it, feed our fiction.

I could live in my imaginary world for a long time, but how boring would those stories become without anything new being added to my world? Even after a long, exhausting day, when everything went horribly wrong, take a moment to make note of the experiences, and your emotions. You can do it either mentally or in a journal. They may not be useful now, but they will be something you can use later, as the seeds grow.

There are also a couple of major draw-backs to having a full time job:

They take up at least eight or nine hours of your day, not to mention the travel time to and from work. And they leave you emotionally and mentally exhausted at the end of the day.

Once we accept both the good and the bad, we can work with them to build that life balance. It isn't going to be easy, and it isn't going to be quick. But you didn't come here for easy or quick, you came here for tools to help change what you're doing. It means saying no, setting yourself as a priority, setting boundaries, taking care of yourself, delegating responsibilities, and setting reasonable expectations.

Self-care is important. Trying to do too much will leave us exhausted, dissatisfied, unhappy, and unproductive. This helps no one. For most of us, we have a knee-jerk reaction to giving ourselves any kind of priority over any one else. It's often why we put off writing in favor of work and family and cleaning the house and looking after the neighbour's garden. If the world revolves around you as much as you think, then it is even more important than ever to take care of yourself. Take five minutes once a day or a few times a week, to take care of yourself. Maybe it's going for a manicure, maybe it's coffee with friends, even better if that coffee is with writer friends where you can simply have a bitch session or a celebratory session as you need it. When we care for ourselves, we feel better, we gain more energy for everything else we have to do.

When you work full time, at a demanding job, you're often exhausted at the end of the day. Often our first instinct is to turn on the TV and veg for 5 hours. Does this really make you feel any better? What might be a better alternative? Something short, something that will help energize you, that will feed your soul? Maybe it's reading a book for 30 minutes, or having a dance party of one in your room to your favourite song or two.

Permit yourself to be a priority, without guilt. You are just as important as everyone else in your life. You deserve time to yourself to pursue your passions. Why should you be the only one not doing something you want to do? Yes, it might make you look bad in other people's eyes, until you have that book launch and you make the local bestsellers list. When I was doing my MA in Writing Popular Fiction at Seton Hill University (it is now an MFA program), it was amazing how much people respected my writing time because it was homework. Once they saw the effort I put into it daily, they have maintained that respect of my writing time. We can't all be so lucky in that way. So now I have to borrow something I fear to admit I heard from Dr. Phil: People treat us the way we teach them to treat us. If we allow others to take time away from our writing, they come to expect that they can do it, that it is okay to do it, that it isn't important to you.

A friend of mine had a sign on her office door, "Do not enter unless it's an emergency." Her son who was sixteen, would come in all the time saying, "You need an emergency hug." Now who can say no to a sixteen year old boy who still wants to hug his mom? But she had to, so that he would stop interrupting her. He started respecting her time and space.

Allowing your writing time to be a priority isn't easy. Setting boundaries are crucial to the process.

Most everyone finds it difficult to say no to others because we don't want them to think badly of us. We like to be needed. We think others won't succeed without us. We need to say no to requests. Our writing time is valuable. Books don't write themselves. And reducing the number of demands on us frees us to be more creative. Next time someone asks you to do something that you know will impose on your writing time, ask yourself if it is really necessary? What will happen if you say no? Will they truly fail without you? To have balance, we have to start saying no.

Sometimes it isn't about saying no to others but saying no to tasks we don't enjoy doing, activities that sap our energy and eat up our writing time. We need to learn to delegate these activities. Are there things in your life that you are doing that you could get others to do? I'm a terrible housekeeper. I know a lot of writers procrastinate by cleaning. I can be in the worst emotional state I've ever been and I will choose to write rather than clean. Recently I decided that even though it stretches my budget, it was time to hire a cleaning service. I'm also not great in the kitchen. I can't hire a full-time personal chef, so I have simple, quick meals. If you're going the self-publishing route and you're not into formatting your manuscript and you know it will take time away from your writing, you can look into hiring someone to do it for you. If grocery stores delivered, (they don't where I live) I would be jumping on that so fast! What about chauffeuring the kids to activities? Can you carpool with some families for kids activities? Can the kids do more of the house-work? You do not have to do everything yourself. Ask others to help out. Remember that support you asked them for as part of your foundation? Here is the practical application of it.

Finding and maintaining balance requires us to know ourselves, to know what we can do, and how much is too much. We need to set ourselves reasonable expectations. We'll talk about this more in a later lesson on goal setting. For now, don't expect that you will write full time if you don't have full time hours to give to it. Don't expect to write 2,000 words an hour if you are a slow typist. Expect that there will be set-backs, but it isn't an all or nothing game. Each day you write, is more than you had the day before. I will challenge you on these expectations shortly. For now, write down what you think are reasonable expectations of your time for writing.

Let's take a moment to look closer at your life balance, and how it can be improved and maintained.

I want you to draw yourself a circle with lines through it like an 8-slice pizza. You can find one of these Life Balance Wheels at the end of the book, and a printable version on my website: http://www.sherrypeters.com/blueprintextras. Name each slice something in your life that takes away from your writing (besides the actual day job). So categories would be things like: family, volunteering, lunch with friends, kids activities, feeling burnt-out at the end of the day, etc.

Rate each of those things on a scale of 1 – 10, 1 is at the centre of the pizza, being it hardly effects you at all, to 10 is the outer edge, being it overwhelms you. Look at the ones that rank above 6. Which of those, if you were to remove them completely from your life, would make everything much easier, much more balanced, and free up time for writing? Ask yourself, what needs to change, to eliminate that stressor from my life? What can you do to make it happen right now? What steps can be taken to remove that stressor in the future?

Now let's move onto prioritization and making writing a priority. I hope you've been keeping track of your daily activities and how much time they take. You're going to start needing that list. Still, don't change anything on that list just yet!

What we choose to spend our time on makes it a priority. If you choose to play solitaire over writing, you're making solitaire your priority. Look at your list of daily activities. What are you spending your time on? When we list the priorities in our life, what we are spending our time on, we can determine which activities we are doing that are important to our goals. We can see what we need to add in, which ones are necessary to our every-day survival, which ones can be deferred, delegated, and which ones can be dismissed all together.

We're going to look at this in terms of spending more time writing as the Big Project. If you're really ambitious, you can make the big project or main goal much bigger, such as signing with a major publisher, being a bestselling indie-author, but let's start with finding time for writing. It is what this book is about :-)

I want you to make a chart, or a list (I prefer lists). You can simply divide a page into four quarters. At the top of the page, write down "Big Project: Writing." Again, I have a Prioritization Chart at the end of this book, and a printable version on my website: http://www.sherrypeters.com/blueprintextras.

In one quadrant, call it Urgent and Important. List all your activities that absolutely must be done and done now. These include replacing the roof after a storm, feeding the two-year old, having morning coffee.

In the second quadrant, call it Urgent and Not Important. List activities that require instant attention, that distract you from your writing time or other activities, things like phone calls, e-mail notifications popping up, kids knocking on your office door.

In the third quadrant, call it Important and Not Urgent. These are activities that don't require our immediate attention, but are what makes our life more fulfilling and help us achieve our Big Project. So these kinds of activities include writing, researching, reading, meeting with other writers, critique group, marketing, coffee with your friends, and date night. You may not do all these things every day, or every week, but they are what rejuvenate you most, and make working toward and achieving the Big Project possible.

In the fourth quadrant, call it Not Urgent and Not Important. These are activities that we spend the rest of our time on. Things that aren't time sensitive, aren't crucial to survival, not uber important to fulfilling your life, and not helpful toward reaching your Big Project. These activities include watching TV, playing computer games; things that we spend our time on to relax or procrastinate.

To achieve your goal of making more time for writing, I challenge you to re-think how you are spending your time. Look at your list of activities. Are you spending most of your time chasing down time-sensitive activities that are wearing you out? Are you able to get help with those activities? What if you were to focus your time and energy more on what is important to you?

Ask yourself the following questions: Where am I spending too much time? Where am I spending too little time? What or who controls my time? How can I gain this control back? What or who causes the most interruptions in my day? How can these be controlled or eliminated? What activity can be eliminated from my schedule? What activity can be delegated or shared with others?

How are you doing with the prioritization? Now let's move on to goal setting and what I like to call Achievable and Exceedable Goals. When we have a full time job and family to look after, we have to be more efficient with our time, which means less dilly-dallying before we get into the actual writing. It means setting more realistic and more focused goals. It also means we may have to be satisfied with getting less work done than we might like. For example, I might think if I can write 1,000 words in an hour, I should be able to do at least 3,000 words an evening. Maybe, but that isn't taking into account the days I struggle with the plot or characters, or have a splitting headache that is making my brain foggy. On those days I might write 500 – 1,000 words. If I'm expecting to write 3,000 words, I'm going to feel miserable. If I expected to only write 500, and I made it to 1,000 words, I would be ecstatic.

Achievable and exceedable goals are the small steps you set yourself en route to completing your project. They fit into your daily routine. They are specific, focused on a single task. And they are measurable in that you will know when it has been achieved.

We all have a tendency to think we can do more than we can in less time than we have. With achievable and exceedable goals, we start with small goals that we know we can complete in the time allotted. Start small and add on if you discover you can do more. Make sure you can achieve your smaller goals first, and be satisfied that you have done your work for the day. And if there are days you can do a little more, that is a bonus.

Someone who has never run before is not going to suddenly be able to run a marathon. First they have to learn how to run properly. They build up their endurance and follow a rigorous training program. If you know you have a big block of time to write coming up, train yourself ahead of time to be disciplined in spending increasing amounts of time writing, and continually increase the word count, but don't expect record breaking results instantly.

Once you have your goals set: the big goals, the long term goals and your short term goals, ask yourself if they are reasonable? Do they fit with your life? Remember that you are shifting your priorities and time schedule to give you more writing time. Keep the daily goals smaller so that you know you will achieve it. Any extra work you do on your project, above and beyond what you had set out to do that day, is a bonus. Build your confidence, know that you can consistently achieve your goals, and exceed them, before pushing for more. But do stretch yourself. Do increase those goals every few days or every week. Look at the minimum number of words you've written in the previous few days, and also at the maximum. Pick a number somewhere in the middle. Aim for it consistently for a week. Then increase it again.

Setting achievable and exceedable goals looks like this: Maybe at first you can only write 500 words a day, or thirty minutes a day, or two hours every Sunday, that's all right. Don't expect more at first. Whatever works for you. We all have a tendency to set unattainable goals. Don't. Start small, build up if you discover you can do more. Make sure you can achieve your smaller goals first, and be satisfied that you have done your work for the day. And if there are days you can do a little more, that is a bonus.

Setting those achievable and exceedable goals is important so let's take a little bit of time here to develop that skill and walk through the process. Guess what? You got it! There's a Goal Setting worksheet at the end of this book, and on my website! http://www.sherrypeters.com/blueprintextras.

We're going to start with the ultimate goal and work our way down through the steps.

What is your ultimate goal? Dream big here. Let your imagination run free. What is it that you really want?

For this example, let's say that we want to be a well-published writer.

That's being fairly modest, not really dreaming big. Okay, I want to be a bestselling author with movies and television series based on my books. I want to go on book tour around the world and live in a palace.

We have the ultimate goal. Now, let's think of the one thing or moment that would symbolize that I have reached the pinnacle of success. Believe it or not, it isn't the palace, the movies, or the around-the-world book tour. My local bookstore has a staircase going up to the second floor. Only the biggest selling authors get to give readings from the staircase. I want to be offered to give a reading from the staircase. Perhaps for you it is being featured on the cover of a magazine or anthology. Maybe it is signing over those film rights to Brad Pitt's movie production company. Maybe it is receiving that first million dollar cheque.

Now ask yourself, what will get you to that pinnacle of success? To be on the staircase at my local bookstore, I need to be a multiple bestseller. To be a multiple bestseller in my genre, chances are high that I'll need to be published by one of the big publishing companies. To get signed by one of the big publishing houses, I'll need to have a reputable agent. To get the reputable agent, I will need to have a marketable and well-written manuscript. To have a marketable and well-written manuscript I can send to agents, I need to have my novel polished and critiqued by trusted readers who will spot not only typos and grammatical errors, but plot and character issues and inconsistencies, and who will help me make this the best book ever. I can't get a novel critiqued if I haven't written it yet. So I have to get writing.

And now for the writing goals. If the final book is to be approximately 100,000 words, by when do I want to have it done? If I think I want to have the book done in a year then I'll have to plan accordingly. The first draft is the most hastily written. At 1,000 words a day, it should take just over 3 months. So let's be generous for extra long work days and maybe a sick day or two and say the first draft will take 4 months. That leaves 8 months for editing, critiquing, more editing, more critiquing, more editing, some more editing, another round of critiques, and some final edits.

Once you have your goals set: the big goals, the long term goals and your short term goals, ask yourself if they are reasonable? Do they fit with your life? If your daily goal is to write for 2 hours every morning before work but you have trouble getting out of bed to get to work on time, you may want to re-think your plan. Either find other times during the day to fit the two hours in, or start by getting up on time for work, then the next week setting your alarm 30 minutes earlier, extending the time each week until you get your 2 hours in. If your plan is to write 2,000 words a day and you have the time to make that word count but you haven't written much more than 100 words a day before, then start with that 100 words a day. Then push yourself to 500 words until you are comfortable with that, then extend it to 1,500 words. But rather keep the goals smaller so that you know you will achieve it and possibly write more as a bonus. Build your confidence, know that you can consistently achieve your goals, and exceed them, before pushing for more. The more consistent you are at writing, the faster the words will come.

How committed are you to achieving these goals? What are you willing to sacrifice to achieve these goals? Remember, it may take years to get a book deal, but when you finally sign, the deadlines come fast and furious, with very little pay. How will you adjust to meeting the annual or semi-annual deadline and still maintain your family life, social life, and work life? What adjustments can you make now so that it will be easier later? You may need to re-prioritize and maybe even eliminate something from your life. Are you willing to spend less time with family and friends if necessary? Are you willing to watch less television? Are you willing to be involved in fewer volunteer activities than others would like?

It is completely up to you how much time and energy you put into reaching your long-term goal, and even in part, the big dream goal. It will take a lot of time and effort. Sacrifices will be made, and you will encounter and deal with a lot of frustration. But it isn't all about sacrifice and punishment. I'm a firm believer in celebrating the little steps as much as the big achievements.

When you have achieved your smaller goals, be sure to treat yourself every now and then. Julia Cameron in The Artist's Way suggests we take artist dates once a week, to replenish the creative well. It is an activity away from your writing, that is just you alone, to let your inner child play. They are great. They don't always have to be her idea of an artist date. A treat for me is often a visit to my local bookstore to look at and maybe pick up a small item like a fun pen or a new journal. Other times it is writing time at a coffee shop. Or a movie. Often, it is simply time to read.

A treat once a week is ideal. Never more, it stops becoming a treat then. But treat yourself. Reward yourself. Celebrate, especially the small steps because achieving the small goals means you are committed and working toward that ultimate big dream goal.

A final note on goal setting. I've asked you to dream big and write down what your ultimate goal and long-term goal might be. For us as writers, these goals are often things like being a bestselling writer, a full-time writer, or having a book contract in a certain amount of time. We want to have these dreams, these goals. Without something to aim for, there is little purpose to our lesser goals. However, it is important to keep in mind that actual publication goals are not within our control. We want to have big dreams to aim for, like a carrot at the end of the stick, perhaps. While attaining them may not be in our control, the goals we set ourselves as steps to put us in a position to achieve our dreams are in our control, and if we do everything we possibly can to achieve our dreams, then we can indeed be satisfied with our efforts and achievements.

All right, I hope you've continued to keep track of you your time usage, because *now* is when we're going to get detailed with it, and start making changes to fit writing into your day!

You've made writing a priority, but you're still having difficulty making time in your day or week for writing. You've gone through your regular activities and figured out which are more important than others, which are more urgent than others. Maybe you don't have the resources to delegate or dismiss certain activities which, if you could, would make spending time on your goals much easier.

Review your time log. Look at the activities you spend your time on. Do you spot any patterns?

Review your goal and priorities. How would you like to spend your time in relation to your goal—the long term goal and short term goals?

Prepare a timeline that will help achieve the goals you've outlined. Draw a timeline with today as the starting point and the completion of the novel as the end point. Write down when you want to have your short-term goals done to achieve your long-term goal. At this point, don't look at your time log. Hey, look! There's even a Timeline worksheet at the end of the book! Oh, and on my website! http://www.sherrypeters.com/blueprintextras.

Now compare your ideal timeline with your current use of time. Examine the gaps, discrepancies, and overlaps between the two. This will pinpoint the differences between your current use of time and your intended use of time. For example, your ideal timeline might have you writing 2,000 words every day, but your current timeline says that two nights a week you're out volunteering or working late which means you won't get those 2,000 words in those days. Your ideal timeline might have you cruising through the 50,000 words in November, but your actual timeline says in November you have a major work commitment, travel for a conference, and five days of Thanksgiving plans and you're hosting this year. What are the reasons for the differences?

Mesh the current use of time with the ideal timeline to create a realistic, workable timeline.

Test out this new timeline for a week or two. Then evaluate how well it worked. Fix what needs to be fixed.

As you review what you spend your time on, are there activities that can be eliminated?

When we have reasonable expectations of our time and can work writing into our schedules and it fits well, it becomes a natural part of our lives, rather than an unsustainable activity with too much stress.

We all know the saying that knowledge is power. The real power comes when you act on the knowledge you have. We can all look at our calendars and schedule in writing time. Sticking to that commitment can be difficult. I hope that with the prioritization and goal setting tools, you will confirm for yourself how committed you are for making time for writing.

I am asking you to make significant changes in your life in order for you to succeed as a writer. It isn't going to be easy. It is natural to resist these changes. Remember what you wrote for the Satisfaction Equation. Remember what you have to gain by implementing these changes. When you make these changes, when you make writing a priority and find the support to keep it a priority, you will succeed.

THE WRITING PROCESS

Your writing process will greatly affect your writing time and your ability to complete your writing project. In this section, we'll be talking about pantsing, plotting (also known as outlining), linear, or random writing processes. I don't believe there is any one writing process that everyone should follow. Plotters tend to be the most militant about it, believing everyone should outline the novel or story to infinite detail before writing. If it works for you, do it. Pantsers, often looked down on with disdain by Plotters, prefer to allow the story to grow around them organically. If you're a Pantser, so called because they discover the story and write it "by the seat of their pants," then great. Do it. Some people have to write their stories from beginning to end, with all scenes written in the exact order they will appear in the final manuscript. Others like to write scenes as they come to them, jumping from place to place in the book and piece it all together at the end.

Whichever works best for you, to help you get the words down in the most efficient way, do it.

I'm going to take this one step further. You may find that whichever process you use might vary depending on what you're writing. You may even find that you are using a combination of all of them. I can hear my Plotter friends shrieking at the horror of my blasphemy!

Perhaps you've been beaten into being a Plotter, or maybe your Pantsing isn't working for you but you're not sure how to switch over. Maybe you're open to exploring new ways of writing. I won't go into great detail about how to do each one, there are much better resources out there for that, but I will go over the positives and negatives of each one which may help you in deciding which one will help you be most successful in getting the words on the page, polishing them up, and getting them out the door.

Pantsing

Pantsing is allowing your story to grow organically, without an outline. Perhaps you start with a character or know the opening scene, or only the theme, and that's all you need to start writing. It is through writing the story that you get to know the characters and the conflict. Stories written by Pantsers tend to be more character-focused stories, full of exploration, where the characters and the conflict are allowed time to breathe and to grow.

Pantsers generally feel that outlining takes out all the fun of writing. The point of writing for Pantsers, is to discover the story as it unfolds. Once you've outlined it, there is no point in writing it because you already know how it ends.

Pantser's stories may to take longer to write. They're more likely to fast draft, where they just write to get the words on the page, and edit later. They may have to go through the story more often to keep consistency and fill in the plot holes.

Plotting

Plotters, on the other hand, feel like pantsing is a waste of time. Their stories tend to be more plot-focused.

There are several ways to be a Plotter. Some Plotters only need to have the opening scene and the climactic moment or end scene, to be enough to consider it an outline. Others have to write down what happens in each chapter or each scene. And others will outline each scene, each character's goal, motivation, and conflict, map plots and subplots, until everything is worked out and all that is left is filling in the description and some dialogue.

Is this more efficient than pantsing? Probably. Certainly when it comes to the actual writing, it takes less time to think about what will happen next because you already know. It also means fewer drafts because you have the consistency and plot holes all figured out so you aren't spending extra time going back to fix problems.

The joy in writing for Plotters, is coming up with a solid plot, a solid story, with rising action and tension, then getting it on the page.

A story by a Plotter may be written faster, but there are times when the outline needs to be revised because the characters or conflict have strayed from the original plan, which can interrupt the flow of writing. However, it is better to revise the outline than force the story to stick to a path that doesn't work.

Linear

Both Plotters and Pantsers can be Linear writers as well. Being a Linear writer simply means that you start writing with the opening scene and go straight through to the end. There may be some plot holes to fill later, or scenes that end up being re-arranged as you edit, but generally speaking, you write straight through to the end.

Writing linearly is great for keeping character and conflict consistent. It keeps the order of events straight in your mind, and character growth in particular. If a character starts off meek but ends up sassy at the end and you write out of sequence, you may end up with a sassy character too early for the story.

On the other hand, if you find yourself figuring out a plot issue for something that happens much later in the story, you may choose not to write it out because that would break up the timeline. I say write it down, you can figure out how it fits into the story later. At the same time, if you figure out that some aspect of the story needs to be changed in earlier chapters, there is no rule saying you can't go back and fix things.

Random

Again, both Plotters and Pantsers can write their projects by writing random scenes then piecing them together through editing. Plotters may find this easier to do as they already have their detailed outline as to what is to happen when, so they have the freedom to write whatever scene they wish to write at that moment. Pantsers can do this as well, though they may have a harder time figuring out how the scenes are to fit together to form a cohesive story. Any writer who writes random scenes may find themselves with excess material, random bits that don't fit, or struggling to write the sequiturs needed to piece it all together.

Writing random scenes can be useful even to the most stolidly linear writer. Any time they feel stuck in one place of the story, they can pick up at any other place in the storyline and continue writing. It can break up the monotony, or help the process of discovery.

Another fun way to be a random scene writer, is to start writing from the end of the story, and working your way to the beginning. Some writers do this as a regular practice, several have tried it as a writing exercise. Again, this is a different way of looking at the story to break out of a rut or feeling stuck, to get a fresh perspective on the story.

Multitasking

Multitasking has been a buzzword in business for years. The more you're able to multitask, the more your boss will approve of you, and the more likely you are at getting a job or promotion.

Multitasking is a myth. You aren't really able to do two or five things at the same time. What you are doing is switching between activities at a quicker rate. And every time you switch activities, you are asking your brain to re-focus its energy and attention. Research is being done to prove that multitasking is detrimental to short-term memory.

So why am I bringing this up in relation to writing? Like Pantsers and Plotters, there are two camps of writers, those who have multiple writing projects going at any time, and those who prefer to focus solely on one project at a time.

Those who have multiple projects going at any given time claim it is more efficient. They have one project on their iPhone that they work on when in line at the grocery store, they have one on their work laptop that they work on during their lunch breaks, they have another one on their home laptop that they work on in the evenings, another one on their desktop they work on in the mornings before the kids get up. If you are able to divide your attention between each one, and easily pick up where you left off with each one, go for it. I suspect this is a really good process for people with ADD or ADHD, who are able to switch focus quite easily. Who actually *need* to switch their focus.

If you aren't able to switch your focus that easily, having more than one or two projects on the go at any given time may not work for you. It will take you longer to get into the story and into the character's minds, eating up the few minutes you have to work on each one.

But there's nothing wrong with keeping your focus on only one or two projects. It can be just as efficient as multitasking. Because rather than spending five minutes a day on one project, and ten on another, and thirty on a third, you are spending all of that time on one project, completing it sooner. The more time you spend on a project, the greater your focus on it, the easier it is to get back into it when you sit down to write.

Instead of dividing your thoughts between projects, you are focusing your excess time allowing your subconscious to fix plot holes and develop character on the one project. It's even better if you are able to find a device that makes your writing portable, that allows you to write at home, on your lunch break, and in line at the store.

THE WRITING

How are you doing? I hope you've started writing. You have your daily word count goals and a deadline to make. You've figured out your writing process or maybe you're playing around with them, seeing which one, or which combination works best for you. It's all good.

Now that you're writing, you get to be creative and live in that imaginary world where you love and torture your characters, build phenomenal magic systems or alien planets, live the hottest romance ever, and explore the deepest heartbreak and betrayal. Now that we've taken care of all the worry about rejection and the business side of writing, we've made time in our schedule for writing, we've made our writing a priority, in theory, this should be the fun and easy part of it all. And often it is.

The first half of the novel is when we truly fall in love with the characters and the story. We're confident that this is going to be a bestseller. That this is the one that is going to get picked up by a big publisher. That this is the one that is going to be our break-out novel.

There is so much potential in each page you write. And you're keen, so you do what you're supposed to do, and you read broadly, and learn from the masters, you go to the bookstore and look at all the books on the shelves and you know exactly where your book will be shelved in close proximity to a big name author which is awesome because that means people browsing for that other author's books will also see yours and will likely pick it up too. You're keen in your writing too. You add subplots and complexity and complications. You've perfected the first few chapters, even tested them on a few other writers for feedback, to confirm that this is the greatest story ever written, and they do confirm it.

And then, and then, and then… you've spent over a month on this thing, and you start to feel that nothing you write matches the awesomeness of the first few chapters. They don't come close. You think maybe you've written in too many complications, too big a world and cast, it's too big for you. You don't feel you're good enough to write this. You're not as good as those big name writers. And then you hear that Veronica Roth was only 25 when her book Divergent hit it big so now the publishers are only looking for young hot writers, and you're 25 too, but you're just starting out, it's too late for you. At a writing conference you go to, you listen to an editor speak about the state of the publishing industry and it is both enlightening and depressing. The worst part is that the editor talks about how they put most of their promotion money into authors who are "marketable," meaning attractive. While you think you look pretty good on any given day, you wonder if you're "marketable" and what would happen to your career if you're not.

You still love your characters and the story and the world, but you start slipping back into those old habits of not making time to write, of making others a priority over your writing. If I were to ask you why you are slipping, you might start making excuses as to why you won't succeed. But this time it isn't your fault, it's everyone else's. Your parents never encouraged you to take a creative writing class, the system worked against you so you couldn't go to University and get a creative writing degree, publishers of science fiction or fantasy don't buy work from women writers because readers don't want it. And they certainly don't want works by writers of non-white ethnicities. You aren't a young supermodel, and even though you're happy with they way you look, it's a global conspiracy to only promote the attractive ones.

So why bother?

Is it really about other people's failings? Or is it really about self-doubt? Protecting yourself, blaming others for what you see as short-comings? Reasons you might get rejected?

When I was a kid, my parents read to my brother and I all the time, especially in the car on summer vacations. On one of these trips, my parents introduced us to the brilliant work of Gordon Korman, whose young adult books are filled with mischief, mayhem, and humour. By this time I'd already decided I wanted to be a writer (I'd decided at age 8 that being a writer was my career choice), so I was curious about this Gordon Korman. What was his story? His first book, a national bestseller, was published when he was sixteen or seventeen. It had been a creative writing project in high school. I knew then and there, that I only had a few years to write my debut masterpiece if I had any hope of being like Mr. Korman, or have anywhere near his success. Well, sixteen came and went and I was still struggling with the writing. I knew by then that I didn't have to be sixteen to make it in publishing. Even so, for the longest time, this niggling thought in the back of my head that said, "It's too late."

It wasn't. It never is. Charlaine Harris had been publishing for twenty years before she broke out with her Sookie Stackhouse novels.

At the end of my grade ten year, I applied to take a creative writing English class the following year. This was an advanced class where you had to submit a piece of writing as part of your application. I was super excited about this class and I was dying of anticipation to know if I got in. You know those scenes in movies or TV shows where someone has auditioned for the school drama or tried out for a team and they all crowd around the door waiting for the list to be posted? That was me and a couple of my friends who had applied. We got in! We were going to learn all the mysteries of how to submit your stories to publishers and magazines. We were on our way to becoming Canada's next great authors!

Take note that this class was to be held the year I was sixteen. I could have been the next Gordon Korman!

I didn't take the class.

I switched schools. The bullying had been overwhelming and I just couldn't take it anymore. I had to get out. So I ended up going to a tiny rural private school with no creative writing program. I kept writing, but it seemed almost hopeless. I'd given up my one chance to learn all the mysteries of the industry and submitting. Because, you know, that information they print in the front pages of magazines that tell you how to submit your story? That couldn't possibly be real. It was too easy. And in my defense, this was before the internet so there were no submission guidelines on publisher websites. But there were books in the library and bookstore called, of all things, Publisher's Market Place, which told you to whom and how to submit your work. I didn't discover that for a few years after high school.

I'd always figured, though, even with the mysteries of submitting solved, I'd missed out on my one opportunity to really learn how to write. Sure I could put sentences together, and I sort of new how to work in conflict and tension and plot, but I always felt like I was missing something.

Was I?

Sure, but it wasn't anything I couldn't have picked up from reading how-to-write books, or simply being more analytical with the books I'd read. I didn't do those things. Instead, for years, I blamed it all on not taking that class, or on the fact I had to drop Creative Writing at University because I had Carpal Tunnel Syndrome at the time and couldn't hold a pen or type.

I did end up going to the Odyssey Writing Workshop in 2005, and later go on to get my Master's degree in Writing Popular Fiction. Were they absolutely necessary to growth as a writer? For me they were. But they aren't for everyone. Yes, I did learn about the craft of writing, and I picked up writing tools I didn't have before. And yet, one of my best friends applied for Odyssey twice and both times got on the waiting list but never attended, and he now has his first book coming out with DAW in March 2016. He thought he needed the workshop, but he didn't.

If you browse the shelves of any bookstore or library and check out the author photos, you will see that people of every ethnicity, weight, or age, are published. If you read their bios, you will learn that authors come from all kinds of socio-political and economic backgrounds. And you will find that most don't have any writing degree; maybe they've taken a course or two. What is the reality of your situation? Do you really need to be a certain age, gender, ethnicity, have a degree?

Find your favourite books on Amazon, and read the reviews. Some are good, some are bad, it is a subjective business. You'll also notice that often the bad reviews are not about the writing, but because the reader didn't like the subject, it didn't match their taste which has nothing to do with your writing, or it is due to things beyond your control, such as its availability, or format. Those aren't valid reviews of your work or opinion of your skill as a writer. Anyone who reads those kind of reviews ought to be able to determine their validity. At any rate, your job as a writer is not to please everyone, it is, first and foremost, to write the story you want to write, and then to please your faithful readers.

I want you to do a survey of books on your bookshelf, at your library or bookstore. Which author did you see who is like you, writing what you want to write? What did they do to get published? What can you learn from their experience and incorporate into your own writing process?

What genre are you most passionate about writing in? What kind of story are you most passionate about telling? Are you writing in that genre? Telling that story? If not, why not? What would it realistically take for you to write in the genre you love, and tell the story you want? If your answer was yes, what is it about the genre you love, about the story you want to tell that makes it your passion?

Who is your ideal reader? What kind of stories do they like to read? Who publishes them? Where do your readers hang out online and in real life? Do they read Traditionally Published books, Indie Published books, or e-books only? Both and all?

Next I want you to write down the excuses you give yourself as to why you might fail. Now write down all the reasons you will succeed.

THIRD FLOOR: THE MURKY MIDDLE AND BEYOND

THE MURKY MIDDLE AND BEYOND

Let's look ahead now to the time when you've been working on the project for a few months, maybe more. Sometimes the writing can be incredibly tedious. It's boring just sitting in your office or on your couch in front of your computer typing, all by yourself, without interaction with friends or family. Maybe the plot isn't working out as neatly as you wanted it to. The characters aren't being as proactive as you think they should be. In fact, they're getting down-right stubborn and refusing to do anything. You've been in this imaginary world maybe a little too long. You've already spent so much time on it and you have so much more writing to do before it is finished. You just want it to be done. You don't want to work on it any more. You're bored, and it is starting to show in your writing.

In books, this is called the murky middle. Rather than there being a climactic turning point in the story, it ends up being filler, where the characters wander the proverbial desert before the next exciting thing happens. That's usually because the writer is bored and doesn't know what to do next, or how to get them there.

For writers, it is also the point in our time with the writing project that the Shiny New idea starts to pop up. The story you're working on has lost its luster. You're no longer convinced it is your break-out novel or even that it is the one that is going to get you the contract. You don't love it so much anymore. The characters are just annoying.

At least they are compared to the Shiny New. A new story with a much more exciting plot and characters and setting, and for sure it will be the break-out, contract-getting, bestselling novel masterpiece you really want to write.

The Shiny New may well be that break-out masterpiece, but more often than not, it is a death-knell for writers. It is what distracts us and draws us away from what we're working on, only to get halfway through another story and be distracted by another Shiny New. It leaves a trail of half-complete manuscript carcasses in its wake.

If success means to get the words down, polish them, and send them out, that implies you have to complete a manuscript to send it out.

You can deal with the Shiny New by taking a couple of hours to make notes, write down as much as possible about it, and set it aside for later, to be the next project.

Then take a look at the deeper concerns that are causing your boredom and need for distraction, which have very little to do with the story you're writing, and work through them.

These deeper concerns have everything to do with our concerns for upsetting family, causing conflict, and the kind of feedback we're starting to get, and connecting with our core values.

Fear of Upsetting People

Family and friends can be wonderful supporters of us but there can also be some tension, some concern that what you write will disappoint them, that they won't approve and so withdraw their support. You do have to live with them and see them at family gatherings and in social situations, after all. What if they read what you write and don't like it? What if you've offended them somehow?

The second novel I ever wrote, was set in Belfast, Norther Ireland, with a working-class protagonist who was a chain-smoker and swore like a sailor. Given where she grew up and lived, this was quite natural for the character. I will admit that I wasn't a huge fan of this character for a long time but she was persistent, and she became one of my favourites. Still is. So I was writing away, smattering the dialogue with f-bombs and more, and I guess my mom peeked over my shoulder (this was many years ago) and caught a few of the curse words. She tutted and said I should write something so crass.

I ignored her, but I could feel her disappointment and it niggled at me for a long time.

Then along came *Mabel the Lovelorn Dwarf* and I'd asked my mom, out of desperation so I could meet a deadline, to proofread the manuscript. She was, well, disappointed, that there were no swear words in it. It was too tame.

I just shook my head and continued to write what I wanted to write. If I had written the way my mom thought I should, or the kinds of stories my great-aunts thought I should—Janette Oke style Christian romances, I wouldn't have been true to the characters, their story, or myself.

Even so, simply writing this section, I'm wondering what my mom is going to think.

When we fear upsetting people, we are worried that they will think we are terrible people because of what we write. We worry that if they don't like our writing, they won't like us.

I can't speak for the average reader who will only know you through your writing, though Social Media and blogs are changing things so that readers feel like they have a personal connection with you, they get to know the real you, not just your books. But family and friends ought to know better.

They ought to know how sweet and funny a person you are, and that the slasher-horror books you write do not change that. You might have a more serious cause for concern if your characters are too similar to family and friends and are portrayed in a negative light. If that's the case, just do a better job of disguising them. Even so, family and friends will always read themselves and others into your work.

It happened to me with Emma, Mabel's best friend in *Mabel the Lovelorn Dwarf*. They were best friends growing up and Emma is blonde. She becomes a nasty piece of work. I was asked if Emma was based on my best friend growing up, who also happened to be blonde. I was stunned, because I hadn't even thought of my friend while I was writing Emma. I had a few other people in mind, but not my friend. The blonde hair was only to contrast Mabel's dark hair.

It happens.

Be true to the characters and the story. You will be happier with your writing. You won't be trying to manipulate things to please others which means the story will flow much better.

Remember that you do not have to show your writing to anyone until you want to. That means family. That means your critique partners too. My family doesn't get to see anything of mine until it is published. They moan about it now, griping that I'm being odd and mean, but that's too bad for them. It is my choice, and always shall be.

I also don't usually let my critique partners see a first draft, or even a second draft, unless I want their input on some plot points.

Fear of Conflict

Fearing what family and friends will think of us because of what we write isn't the only fear that gets in the way of our writing, creating the murky middle and the advent of the Shiny New. A big one is the fear of conflict.

A lot of this has to do with the amount of time it takes to write the story. Writing takes time. The more time we spend with our writing, the less time we're spending with family and friends. And they're starting to make demands of us. They ask us to help them with something, attend events, or spend time with them, when they knew we had set aside that time for writing.

The fear makes us feel bad for wanting the time for ourselves. It convinces us that our family and friends will not understand, that they'll feel like we're neglecting them, which will create conflict and because we don't want conflict, we set aside our project to do what is asked of us.

There is the direct application of this fear, which is when family and friends ask us to spend time with them. "Let's go for coffee" can seem so harmless. We think it's just coffee, or lunch, or just an extra hour. We don't want to disappoint our friends or family even though we would rather, or know we need to be writing. We have already said "no" to them a lot and they're whining that we never have time for them anymore. We're worried if we keep saying "no," they'll stop inviting us out. Our kids demand our attention and we don't want them to throw a tantrum the neighbours can hear, so we put aside what we are doing to play with them even though we've just spent five hours with them and asked for one hour to ourselves, and they're supposed to be napping.

Remember my friend's sixteen year old son who would disturb her while she was writing, even though she had a sign on her door that said "Do not disturb unless it's an emergency." He'd burst in, saying she needed an emergency hug" While sweet and adorable, it was distracting, taking away from her time, and she gave in because she didn't want there to be conflict. She ended up having to change the sign to "Do not disturb unless there's blood or fire." It helped.

So we start to feel guilty and spend more time with family and friends and less time on our writing. When we spend less time with our writing, we stop being in that head-space, we lose our focus, we lose the excitement of writing. But we feel bad about it and so we start to look for something new to bring back that excitement, to renew our love of writing.

It isn't just the demands of family and friends that make us feel bad about taking time for our writing. There is also the more subtle implication that taking time for writing is wasting our time. I mean it takes, what, a whole year to write a book, or longer? And that's before you even attempt to sell it. Where are your results? What have you got to show for all your hard work and the long hours you're putting in?

It's why we feel more productive playing games than we do writing. At least with a game you go up a level, you win points, and maybe even some bonus rewards. With writing, it is hours of more words on the page, and that doesn't feel like proof of accomplishment so then we feel like we're wasting our time.

So much in today's society is results oriented. Take up running and keep trying to beat your time. Study in school, but only what will be on the test. Give progress reports at work. Unless you're providing tangible results with you're writing, it still feels like it is "just a hobby" and a hobby is what you do when you have nothing better to spend your time on.

And so you clean the house, and do the dishes, and you go to the gym a few hours a day, and put in overtime hours at work, because that gives you visible results that people can make note of and approve of and therefore approve of how you're spending your time.

In the meantime, you've lost interest in what you were writing, you feel bad about it, and are looking for something new and exciting to restore that love of writing. Something that screams "This will be worth spending your time on!"

CONNECTING WITH OUR CORE VALUES

Neither the fear of upsetting people nor the fear of conflict are necessarily conscious fears. They are simply our natural instinct for survival. But we don't have to give in to them or get distracted by the Shiny New, to avoid extinction. We can move through the murky middle and complete our novel by re-connecting with our core-values and through that, set and hold boundaries.

Our core values are why we do what we do. They are the deep-down motivation behind everything. This goes back to the Foundation you built. It is about why you write, and why you are writing this book. Take out those lists now and remind yourself of why you write, and what your goals were when you started this project. What, if anything, has changed? What else can you add to that list? Now that you've spent so much time on this project, what have you learned about yourself and the theme you're writing about? What is the real reason you're writing this story?

It is also very much worth taking some time to remind yourself about why you write. Why you want it to be more than a hobby. To find the true value of writing for you, we need to go a little deeper. To do so, there are a series of questions that can be asked and answered.

For myself, one of the reasons I write is because I love to explore other view-points. It's a fairly vague reason for writing, it applies to most anything I write. Which is good. But why is exploration of other perspectives important to me? It broadens my mind and makes me more open and accepting of others. Why is being more open and accepting of others important to me? Because I think it's important to live in a society where we don't judge each other. If there was less judgment, there would be less conflict. And why is less judgment and less conflict important to me? If there is less judgment, then I won't be judged. And if I'm not judged, what does that mean for me? It means I am accepted. Therefore, one of the core values of me choosing to be a writer, is that through my writing, I gain acceptance, of myself, and of the larger population.

There are other reasons for why I write that would lead me to a core value of joy, and simply being who I am supposed to be.

The same can be done for the reasons why you write what you write.

My novel is important to me because the theme is a social issue I am passionate about.

The theme gives me a release for my passion.

The release gives me a sense of making a difference in the world.

Making a difference gives me a feeling of rightness.

That rightness makes me feel mentally balanced.

Feeling mentally balanced gives me inner peace.

Inner peace gives me joy.

Core value: Joy

Try it a few times. What are your core values?

When we re-connect with our core values, our works-in-progress which seemed so tedious and murky, has regained that shine, renewed our affection, and our keenness to tell that story. We want to spend time on it. We no longer see it as a waste of time. We see that our results will come later, and that's OK. Our house gets a little dirty, the dishes don't get done right away, and that's all right. The guilt goes away. We stop worrying about what our family and friends will think about us, and we have fewer problems saying no to their requests.

By the time you are finished that story, you will be ready to move on to the next, but you will have completed your project and well on your way to success.

But let's not stop here. Let's take a few minute to reinforce your writing as a priority, by setting and keeping boundaries.

When you love your writing, it is much easier to make it a priority. And you're back on the word-count schedule so you're well on your way. Still, there will be intrusions. Family and friends will continue to make requests and demands and if we're not careful, we can slip back into the pattern of guilt.

Boundaries are necessary to help us achieve our goals. Boundaries are difficult. I don't know anyone who is always perfectly capable of building and maintaining their boundaries. But it is still worth the effort.

Remember my friend whose son would come give her emergency hugs? Her office door being closed and the do not disturb sign had been her boundary. When she was in the office, she was supposed to be left alone. Her son found a loop-hole and exploited it. When she changed the do not disturb sign on her door, she reinforced that boundary, making sure her son did the same.

An important part of keeping those boundaries, is respecting them ourselves. If we say we're going to be spending Saturday morning in our office writing and no one should disturb us, then spend Saturday morning in your office writing, not out of the office, watching TV with the kids. If we respect our boundaries, others will learn to as well.

A couple of writer friends of mine told a great story about family respecting boundaries. I'm going to paraphrase here and alter a few of the details, mostly because I can't remember it word for word. Steve's writing time was Saturdays. On Saturdays, the kids were told, Dad is invisible. He isn't here. You cannot go to him for help or for a chit-chat. On Saturday's, Dad doesn't exist. So one Saturday afternoon, one of his daughters is in a big high school basketball game, and being the loving father that he is, Steve goes to the game. His daughter's team wins and afterwards she comes up to the family and hugs her mom and brothers and sisters but not Steve. She doesn't even look at him. She celebrates a little with her family and then goes off to be with her teammates. Steve's a little hurt by this. So when the daughter gets home, he asks her about it, and she says, "But Dad, it's Saturday. You're invisible on Saturdays."

His boundaries had been set and respected for so long, that the family maintained it, even on the one day he didn't. That takes commitment to teach the family to be that way.

But boundaries aren't always about family and kids. There are always organizations looking for volunteers and community groups expecting involvement. Saying no to others is difficult. It isn't in our nature. We want to be helpful, to be seen as useful and community-minded, not selfish.

Saying no is *crucial* to be a writer.

Once you've been published, there will be other opportunities, like newspaper and television interviews, speaking engagements, conventions and conferences you'll be invited to attend, high school and university students asking for help with the essay they have to write about your work, and fans wanting to have an hour or two or ten of your time. You'll want to say yes to all of it. It's all good publicity, isn't it? To say yes to everything, means much less writing time. And without the writing, there will be nothing to promote.

Books don't write themselves. I wish they did, but they don't. We *have* to say no. It is OK to say no. If we don't, we spend too much time away from our writing.

We often feel like we have to say yes because if we don't the person asking for our help won't find anyone else, the organization needing our volunteer time won't have enough volunteers and therefore won't be able to function.

I hate to break it to you, but at the same time I hope you find this liberating: You're not that indispensable. The world will function without you.

It's harsh. I know. We all believe the world revolves around us and to find out it doesn't, can be soul-crushing. The good news, though, is that now that the world doesn't revolve around you, you are free to say no, to spend time writing, and know that the others will be all right. They may complain and whine, they may lay a heavy guilt-trip on you, but I promise, they will be fine. And they might surprise you and not realize that they are asking too much of you and will turn around and offer you support.

It will be tough, but worth it, when you have that completed manuscript that you've polished and start sending out.

GETTING FEEDBACK

All right! You're past the murky middle, you've completed the manuscript and now you're starting to polish it up before you send it out. An important part of this process is getting feedback. You don't want just any feedback though. You want it to be critical but helpful.

Receiving feedback on our work-in-progress is a huge part of the writing process. We spend so much time on the manuscript that we stop seeing what can be improved so having others read it over helps give us perspective on our writing. Every writer does it, whether it be through a writer's group or beta-readers—they all receive feedback on their writing to improve the manuscript before submitting or publishing.

Choose who you want to see your work. If you're worried about the response from your family and friends, they don't have to see it. Family is supposed to give the unconditional love feedback, no matter what you write, that it's wonderful, dear. If they won't do that, they don't get to see it. The people you want to see it are other writers who are of the same or preferably higher caliber of writing than you are. They don't have to be writing in the same genre as you, though it helps if they are, but a mix of genre writers is good to provide other perspectives. The point is, you get to choose who sees your work at which stage.

When looking at receiving feedback, there are a few things to keep in mind. It is important to have trusted readers who are knowledgeable in the craft of writing to read over our work, point out what we are doing well and where we need to improve. Not only can they point out grammatical and spelling errors, but plot issues we've missed, confusing dialogue, character discrepancies, inconsistencies, and where we need more world-building. Receiving feedback from trusted readers is what makes our writing the best it can possibly be, and ready to submit it to agents and editors.

One of the best, and most consistent, ways to get feedback, is to join a critique group. It isn't always necessary to have a critique group as long as you have a number of readers who will provide you with similar feedback.

There are different kinds of critique groups. There are online groups where you can post a story or chapters of your novel and a number of the other members will give you feedback. These usually work on a point system. The more critiques you yourself give, the more critiques you are entitled to receive. And then there are the in-person critique groups of usually three to seven members, sometimes more. Depending on the group needs will determine how often you meet and how many pages you can submit each time. And everyone critiques everyone else's work.

Make sure that the other writers in your group have the same end-goal. If your ambitions are not aligned, conflict may arise in giving and receiving critique. For example, if you are looking to improve your craft but not to submit, make sure the others are after the same thing. If you want your manuscripts to be submission ready, fellow writers who are also after submission and publication will know what to look for to help you.

Anytime you send your work to someone for critique, make sure that their feedback will be helpful. You absolutely want to hear what you are doing right, but you also want to know what you are doing wrong and where you need to improve. If you do not find the feedback helpful, find other people to critique with

So what is appropriate, honest, but tough feedback? There are loads of articles out there about how to give feedback, but here are a few key points. Don't say you like something if you don't like it. If something amazing pops out at you, say so, and why, what is it about that sentence or scene that worked for you. You can be critical, but make sure you're being helpful. Don't say something is stupid or terrible and leave it at that. Tell the author why you thought the character wouldn't say or do what they are doing, tell the author why the scene didn't work for you. And most importantly, you are critiquing the writing, not the writer. Just as you don't want to be judged based on the content or quality of your writing, so you are not to judge others based on the same.

It is natural, when receiving feedback, to feel defensive. After all, you have spent a lot of time and hard work on your writing, it is your baby, and now someone is pointing out that your baby is not as beautiful as you thought it was. I have an automatic response when I am defensive which is that clearly these people do not get my genius, and mores the pity for them. I only allow that defensiveness to last for a moment because I don't want it to get in the way of my growth as a writer. Whatever your defensive instincts are, do not let your defensiveness prevent you from being open to the helpful advice being offered. Usually the people I thought least understood my genius are the ones who truly got it and want it to shine.

When you have several people critiquing a piece of your writing, you are free to take all or nothing or some of the advice. It is your story, after all. Not everyone will have the same interpretation of the story and will have varying suggestions. It is up to you to decide the best direction for your story. A general rule of thumb is that if fifty percent or more of your critiquers suggest you make a certain change, you should give that suggestion great consideration. But if you find only one person commented on something but you find that feedback helpful, you can choose to go with it. I'll say it again: it is your story. You know what is best for it. If you can reasonably defend why you wrote something the way you did, you should keep it in.

When you review the feedback, also look at what has not been said. For example, if you receive comments that want to take the story in a different direction than you intended, it may in fact be that you need to make something clearer. An example of this happened to me when I was first writing Mabel the Lovelorn Dwarf. I had been writing several short stories with the characters for a few years before I attended Seton Hill University and decided to write a novel about them. My first attempts at the novel were terrible. I knew the characters too well. The stories I had written took place later than the starting point of the novel, so in my mind, they had already grown and changed and yet I was writing them in situations where they would have been in different emotional and mental places. Mabel is the protagonist, and Emma is the antagonist, and yet, the way I was writing them, Emma was clearly the more sympathetic character. All my critiques said that they liked Emma better than Mabel. That Mabel was horrible. For a while, I kept changing the situations they were in. It didn't help. I didn't understand why everyone loved Emma. It took me a while to read between the lines. It wasn't the situations I was putting them in, it was that I thought of them differently. When I changed them, to be more like they had been when they were younger, the story worked.

Most importantly, be open to feedback. Use it to your advantage, to your growth and development as a writer. It is not a judgment of you as a writer. It is meant to make your work-in-progress the best it could possibly be.

They say it takes a village to raise a child. Well, if your writing is your baby, your critique partners and beta-readers are the villagers helping you. Not by judging you but by enhancing your skill-set.

FOURTH FLOOR: GOING PUBLIC

GOING PUBLIC

Success is getting the words down, polishing, and sending them out. The Fourth Floor, is sending out those pages! You've done it! You've completed your novel or story, and now it's time to send it out.

With the ever-fluctuating publishing industry, there are so many more options open to writers that it can be overwhelming. There is also more work for writers to do in terms of promoting themselves, and our fears of failure and success are as strong as ever.

After you send your writing out the door, you are no longer in control of what happens to it. You cannot control who will buy it, and you cannot control the response times. What you can control, is who you send it to, how you promote yourself, and which direction you decide to go as an author. And it is those last few items that we control that we'll focus this last section on, starting with the debate over Indie v. Traditional.

Indie v. Tradition Publishing

This is not going to be one of those debates where I militantly tell you you have to go one way or the other. There are a lot of pros and cons to both, and you should be aware of what some of them are so that you can make the decision that's best for you. Because really, it's your choice. What works for one author doesn't necessarily work for another. You may want your writing career to go one way, I may want mine to go another. And that's all right.

For the most part, I'm going to have to speak in generalities because the industry is always changing and I'm sure that in a year from now, or less, this chapter is going to be completely obsolete. I am also aware that there are exceptions to the rules, but they are exceptions, outliers, they are not the majority of cases that make up the rules, they prove the rule exists for a reason.

So here we go.

Why should you choose the Traditional Publishing route. Chances are, it has been your dream to be published by one of the big publishing houses, to see the Penguin logo on the spine of your book, and for your work to be available in all the major bookstores. You get those things if you go the traditional publishing route.

You get publicity. Newspapers and major online review sites will review your book. Publishers pay for advertising space. It may be limited in the amount of advertising they pay for, but it is their expense, not yours. Their publicity department may set you up for interviews with news outlets or TV appearances, and they may send you on a book tour, although the latter is becoming rare, but they'll also pay for your book launch party in your home city.

The publisher looks after all the tiny little details. As a writer, your job is to send them the manuscript. Your agent will look after the contract and the financial details. Your agent will sell foreign rights and movie and TV options and rights as well. The publisher will worry about the interior layout, the typesetting, the cover art and design, which you may or may not have input on. They find other authors to blurb your books.

They will edit your book. Yes, your job is to send them a manuscript that could go straight onto the bookshelf, and often that's the case, but sometimes, the editor will actually make editorial suggestions. At the very least, you will have a copyeditor to look for typos and consistency and spelling errors.

Of course, the big reason to go to a Traditional Publisher, is that you get paid. There's a saying that professional writers have long abided by: Money flows to the writer, not away from the writer. You get paid an advance, and when your advance earns out, you get royalties.

There are a few caveats to what I've just said. Book tours are rare, so don't count on it. Generally, you have to be one of the bigger names in publishing to get a book tour. The same thing with TV appearances and interviews. Unless you are a big name, or write about a hot topic that can jump out at the media as being a story other than what your book is about, it likely isn't going to happen. The advances for first novels are generally quite small, they are broken up into two, three, or even four payments, and because they haven't invested a whole lot in your advance, they aren't going to advertise a whole lot. There likely won't be any end-caps at bookstores for a while. So if your advance is $5000, and your royalty rate is 10% for your mass-market paperback (which is a high royalty rate, it would be more like 8%), then you have to sell 500 copies before you start earning royalties.

But this is all for writers starting out. If you prove to be an author who can build a following, have bigger readership, then you will get bigger advances, you will get those end-caps, you will get a book tour and publicity appearances.

Small presses are becoming a more viable option, especially if you write something a little different. You won't earn as much in an advance, but you may get more personable treatment, and a lot of small presses have great reputations, along with the distribution abilities of the bigger houses.

If the publishers and agents take care of all of the details and financial stuff, and small presses are an option, why on earth should anyone consider self-publishing, or indie publishing as it is called?

You have control over the layout of your book, you get to pick your cover artist and cover design. It's time consuming, but all the decisions are yours. You have control over the e-book distribution as well, allowing you to have your book available in outlets such as Smashwords, which traditional publishers don't use.

The Traditional Publishing industry is constantly changing. Most of the publishing houses are run by corporations who aren't so much concerned with the creative side of books. Their only concern is the bottom line. They will invest in authors like Dan Brown and James Patterson and Stephen King, because they know they will bring in money. They aren't necessarily keen on bringing in new writers unless they can already deliver a big audience. It's why you see so many books in the bookstore that are so similar. If you write something that is a little bit off the beaten path of what has been proven to sell, you are less likely to get picked up. Not because your writing isn't good, they just don't see it as marketable, meaning it doesn't hit the mainstream of what is out there. Independent publishing is allowing all kinds of authors to write the stories they love to write, that aren't sparkly vampires in high school, and find their own market, and some are doing rather well by it, financially.

The money is a big reason as well. So traditionally, as I said earlier, it has been said that money flows to the writer, not away from the writer. Personally, I still think that should be true, but given the market climate, that isn't the case any more. Independent publishing has become an economically viable option. There are the up-front costs that the author has to pay for like an editor (please, if you're reading this book then I know you want to take your writing career seriously, please, please, please, invest in a good editor, no matter how many beta readers you have), and cover art. Professionally edited writing will be a better product, a professional looking cover will help sell your work. There are a few good options for getting print books. A lot of people use CreateSpace. I've used Lightning Source. Both are print on demand. You can order as few or as many books as you want. You no longer have to have your basement full of books that you've paid thousands of dollars for. Lightning Source is owned by the Ingram distribution company so when you go through them, your books are automatically listed on Amazon and Barnes and Noble, and Chapters.

We're not done talking about the finances. Now that you've spent the money, you can see it come in. You may not sell as many books, but you will make much more per book than the traditionally published author. Payments on e-books for the independent author, are 70%. So your e-book selling at $2.99, earns you $2.10. My print books earn me 70% minus the printing costs. I order a few boxes of my own books and aside from paying the shipping and printing costs, they are mine. I sell them at a slight discount at conventions and conferences, all the money is mine.

W00t! I'm rich! Not quite. There are plenty of downsides to Indie-publishing. There are all the up-front costs and having to do all the work yourself, paying for your own publicity. Newspapers and major online reviewers, will not review your book. Bookstores will not carry your book unless you go in and personally sign a consignment agreement. Barnes and Noble does have a process where you can send some copies of your books to New York and they will review it before agreeing to carry them in some of their stores.

You have to build your own following. At least with Independent publishing you aren't expected to hit the bestseller list or be a big earner with your first couple of books. You are allowed to build that following. The more books you have out, the better. Most readers of Indie books, tend to devour them rather quickly, meaning the more prolific you are, the better. This can reduce the quality of your books because you're trying to put them out every 3 - 6 months. But you also have the freedom to say, "No, I'll only put them out every 6 - 12 months." It will take you longer to build a name and earn the money.

Which one should you chose? Go with your gut. If your dream is to be published by Penguin, write the best damn book you can, find an agent, and give it a try. Be aware that it can take years before you get an agent, and it could be longer before you get a book contract. So keep writing new and better books and submit them too. If you've exhausted the traditional route, then try Indie publishing. It can't hurt. If you don't want to wait, and you don't mind putting in the work and making the initial investment, go the independent route.

Marketing

I know I talked briefly about marketing earlier, but it is worth talking about again, because it is a big part of going public with your work. Whether you are Traditionally or Independently published, you will have to market your self and your work.

Rule number one, is, always has been, and forever will be, write the best books you can.

Start building your following on Facebook, Twitter, Instagram, Pintrest, and your blog. Agents and editors will look at that. No, you don't have to do all platforms of social media, but you should have at least a blog and one or two forms of social media interaction.

Be on the internet occasionally, but not all the time. Most of your time should be spent writing, remember? But when you are on social media and blogging, be yourself. Blog about what you're passionate about. Don't constantly post about your book, that gets annoying really quick. The people who follow you, who will be your readers, want to feel like they know you personally. If you're an Indie Author, for the love of all that is good in this world, if someone follows you on Twitter and Facebook, DO NOT send them an instant message telling them where they can buy your book. They will unfollow you in a heartbeat. If you wish to acknowledge their follow, simply tweet "Thank you (insert name here) for the follow", or on Facebook "Welcome new follower (insert name here)." It will make them feel a part of your inner circle and acknowledged by you.

Fear of Rejection / Fear of Success

We talked about fearing rejection when we talked about dreaming big, back on the first floor. At that point we talked about rejections not being personal, and not self-rejecting our work. But here we are, we have successfully completed a novel, a story, we've spent countless hours on it, we've neglected our family to work on it. It is done! And now it is time to send it out. And now we start to fear that all that time, all that effort, all that neglect, will have been for nothing. What if we send it out and every agent or editor tells us our work it isn't marketable, it isn't what they're looking for. Each editor or agent has the possibility of being like Simon Cowell and telling us we should never write again.

So we start to make excuses. It isn't really ready, it needs more editing, you need to do more research on the right market (even though you've spent months on it already). You don't have a big enough online platform so you need to spend more time building it first

What about this fear of success? Is that really a thing? It is. An acceptance doesn't just mean a paycheque. Your life will change. There will be hard and fast deadlines. You'll have to market yourself. People are going to read your work and have opinions on it, which might not be positive! Success of an acceptance can also bring out the fear of being discovered, you fear that you are an imposter; that this one story was a fluke, that you can't really write.

So we start to make excuses. It needs more editing, you need to do more research on markets to submit to, you need to build more of an online platform.

At first glance, these two fears appear completely opposite, but their sources are the same: the fear that you're not good enough and that it was all a waste of time.

To complete our definition of success, we have to send our work out into the world. To do so, we have to believe in ourselves This isn't about being confident in our work, it is about being confident in ourselves as writers, that this one story is just the beginning, that we have more stories in us, that we have the ability to continue to grow as writers, to learn, and to have something to say.

It is time to believe in yourself. Take a moment to look back at all that you have done to complete this project. How many hours have you dedicated to it? What have you learned about the theme? What have you learned about the writing craft? Look back at the list you created at the beginning of the project about why you wanted to write it. How many of those have you achieved? How many more reasons have there been for writing it that you added to the original list? Look at all those smaller goals you set yourself to complete this project. You have achieved all those smaller goals to reach this bigger one.

You did it. No one else. You worked hard to accomplish it. No one else. You could have given up but you didn't. You have, inside you, the drive and determination to work hard, to achieve your goals.

Having it rejected does not mean you wasted all that time and talent. Not sending it out would mean all that that time and talent has been wasted. Having it accepted will change your life, but that is what you want. You are not an imposter, your drive and talent and work-ethic proves it.

Look at the feedback you have received from your critique partners that have helped made the story better, but also pointed out what you do well.

Send out your story, and start writing another one. Prove to yourself how much you have grown as a writer. Prove to yourself that you have more stories within you. Prove to yourself that you have what it takes to make it as a writer.

ROOFTOP GARDEN: CELEBRATE!

CELEBRATE!

We all respond positively to reward. Rather than setting up punishments for not reaching certain milestones, set up rewards for reaching them.

If you had been told as a child that you had to eat your brussels sprouts or you wouldn't get dessert, you probably shoved them into your mouth, swallowed them, and scowled at your parents. If, however, you were told, if you eat your brussels sprouts, then you'd get dessert, you'd probably do it with a little more cheer. The reward is exactly the same, it is the wording that changes our attitude. And when we do things with a little more cheer, we tend to want to do better, do more, or be a little quicker.

So rather than work away from a punishment, let's work toward a reward.

I also believe in celebrating the small steps. Writing is a long and often tedious process. Sure, people celebrate with us when we make a sale, or sign a book contract. But we also need to celebrate finishing a draft, or mastering a new part of the craft and integrating it into our writing, or finishing each chapter, or meeting our word count goals for each week. It is these rewards that keep us wanting to go back to the hard work of putting words on the page in the hopes of a sale somewhere down the road.

Every time you achieve one of the small steps: Celebrate.

Every time you work on your project when you didn't think you could: Celebrate.

Every time you feel that joy and satisfaction from the project: Celebrate.

Every time you commit to your project regardless of the potential conflict it might cause: Celebrate.

You see, it is important to celebrate the small steps, not just the big finale. Celebrate by doing something small for yourself, like taking yourself to a movie, or a trip to your favourite shop, or out for a special coffee at Starbucks. It can also be simply time to yourself. Whatever you do, make sure it is away from your project. Whatever you chose, make it time for your inner child to play.

A treat once a week is ideal. Never more, it stops becoming a treat then. But treat yourself. Reward yourself. Celebrate, especially the small steps because achieving the small goals means you are committed and working toward your dream.

FINAL THOUGHTS

FINAL THOUGHTS

This is an ongoing process. With the changes you have made and more changes you are considering, your productivity, getting the words on the page, should have already increased, and will continue to do so.

There will be days when things don't go as planned. You will have hard days at work and take the evening off and feel guilty about it the next day because you know you should have been writing. There will be times when you let your boundaries slip and agree to volunteer for some activity even though you know it will take away from your writing time.

That's OK. We all have our off days. Start fresh the next day. Prepare yourself a time log for each week, with your writing time blocked off. Remind yourself of your goals—the small ones and the big one. This isn't a diet where one off day of eating cake and pie and cookies negates months of work. You have already made great progress. Put the off day behind you.

Don't let your Inner Saboteur convince you that because of the bad day yesterday, you've blown it all so don't bother writing today. If you listen to that negativity, one off day will turn into an off week which will turn into an off month. You have the tools to get right back at the writing without straying from the plan. You *can* do it. I have faith in you. You put in the work to create your blueprint. Have faith in *yourself*.

You will also find that as your life circumstances change so does your blueprint. Your reasons for writing will change. Your support system will change. Your writing passions will change. But so will your family situation. Kids grow up. Jobs change. Moves happen. Go back to the tools in this book, and tweak them as you need to.

This is all about *your* personal success as a writer. Your timelines are not the same as anyone else, nor should they be. We are all individuals with very different lives and very different end goals. For someone it may be to complete a novel in 6 months. For someone else it might be to complete a novel in a year or two.

At the same time, don't let yourself get away with things or going to easy on yourself. Demand more. You *can* do more than you originally believed. Start small with your goals, but push yourself to increase them. Then tweak your blueprint to solidify those new goals.

Grow your goals, and challenge yourself to continue to grow as a writer.

Enjoy the process of writing. Live in the moment of your story and fall back in love with the characters, the conflict, the world. Fall in love with the editing process, of reconstructing the sentences, of making each line more powerful, to say what you really wanted to say. Enjoy writing what you are most passionate about. Let your passion show in your writing.

And of course, celebrate!

To that end, I want to offer you a couple of bonuses as a reward for completing this book!

The first bonus: visit my website and sign up for my newsletter which will, on occasion, have bonus writing success material and other special offers. When you sign up for my newsletter, you will receive *10 Keys to Perseverance*. As an extra extra, you will also receive the first few chapters of my other book, *Silencing Your Inner Saboteur*. If you've forgotten, my website is http://www.sherrypeters.com.

The second bonus is that of a complementary 45 minute coaching session. As a coach, I help my clients be accountable, I help them figure out their goals, priorities, time management, and help them to decide what changes need to be made and how to make them. If you would like to delve further into the issues raised in this book and you would like to see if coaching is right for you, send me an e-mail at sherypeters@outlook.com, and we'll set something up. I would love to work with you and see you succeed.

Happy Writing!

Sherry

JOURNAL QUESTIONS

FOUNDATION

Why do you write?

What inspires you to write?

What do you love about writing?

What are the practical reasons you write?

What makes this writing project worth your time, and energy?

Why are you willing to give up time you could be spending with family and friends, on this project?

What are your reasons for writing this specific story?

What do you hope to personally gain from this story?

What you want to gain professionally from writing this story?

What is your current pre-writing routine?

How can you make it portable?

What will work in line at a grocery store, at a coffee shop or lunchroom, and at a writing retreat?

BLUEPRINT FOR WRITING SUCCESS

What is the end result you're after?

What do you want?

What do you really want?

What do you need to do to get there?

What will you do to get it?

What you will do today towards your goal?

Who supports you?

Are you part of a writers group or other writing organization? If not, where can you find that support?

What can you do to show your family how important writing is to you?

DREAMING BIG

What do you want your writing career to look like?

What kind of book or story do you want to write?

What is the theme of your book?

How elaborate and complicated do you want the plot to be?

How many characters do you want in the story?

What are their personalities like?

After the one story or book, are you done writing?

Is that enough? If not, what do I really want? Not tomorrow, but five, ten, or maybe twenty years from now. What do I want my writing life to look like?

Forget publishing trends. Don't try to guess what the editors of a themed anthology are looking for. What is the story you want to tell?

Is that really what you're passionate about?

When you decided to submit to that anthology, what was the first idea to pop into your head? What was it that connects with you, that made you think "I could submit something for that?"

For your novel or other short stories, think about why you write, what you're passionate about. What do you have to say to your readers.

Take a moment and think about past projects you didn't complete. You stopped working on them for any number of reasons. What were those reasons?

What was your skill level then?

Were you passionate about it?

Did you have the knowledge you needed, or access to it?

What makes this project different from the others?

What makes *you* different from when you worked on those other projects?

Make a list of all the writing classes you've taken, or writing books you've read and learned from.

What are the most important things about writing that you learned from each one?

Think about what you knew about writing when you first decided you wanted to write a story, any story. How much more do you know now?

Think about what makes the story you are writing unique to you.

After completing the Internal/External Reference worksheet, how does this change things for you?

Where do you see yourself in five years?

Ten years?

Twenty years?

What can you do right now to make this happen?

What do you need to do, to make it happen?

What needs to change, for it to happen?

What classes do you have available for you to take to develop your craft?

What writing books do you need to read, actually read them, not just buy them and have them sit pretty on your bookcase?

What do you really want?

Yes, it will take time, and sacrifices will have to be made. Is the dissatisfaction, vision, and clarity, greater than your resistance to change?

What if it is worth it and you decided not to pursue it?

What if you do pursue it and you reach your dreams?

What if you decide not to pursue it, and nothing changes for you?

GETTING TO WORK

Looking at your Life Balance Wheel. Of the items rated higher than 6, which one, if you were to remove it completely from your life, would make everything much easier, much more balanced, and free up time for writing?

What needs to change to eliminate that stressor from your life?

What can you do to make that happen right now?

What steps can be taken to remove that stressor in the future?

You've completed the Achievable and Exceedable Goals. How committed are you to achieving these goals?

What are you willing to sacrifice to achieve these goals?

It may take years to get a book deal, but when you finally sign, the deadlines come fast and furious, with very little pay. How will you adjust to meeting the annual or semi-annual deadline and still maintain your family life, social life, and work life?

What adjustments can you make now so that it will be easier later?

Do you really need to be a certain age, gender, ethnicity, have a degree to be a writer?

Do a survey of books on your bookshelf, at your library or bookstore. Which author did you see who is like you, writing what you want to write?

What did they do to get published?

What can you learn from their experience and incorporate into your own writing process?

What genre are you most passionate about writing in?

What kind of story are you most passionate about telling?

Are you writing in that genre? Telling that story? If not, why not?

What would it realistically take for you to write in the genre you love, and tell the story you want?

If your answer was yes, what is it about the genre you love, about the story you want to tell that makes it your passion?

Who is your ideal reader?

What kind of stories do they like to read?

Who publishes them?

Where do your readers gather, online and off?

Write down the excuses you give yourself as to why you might fail.

Write down all the reasons you will succeed.

THE MURKY MIDDLE AND BEYOND

Core Values:
In one sentence, what does writing do for you?

What does the above answer do for you that is even more important?

Keep taking each answer and asking what it gives you that is even more important to you, until you get to a one word answer. Do the same for the project you are writing.

Example:
Writing lets me explore other worlds.
That exploration gives me a sense of adventure.
Adventure gives me a sense of openness.
Openness gives me etc.

Continue your Core Values Exploration.

GOING PUBLIC

Look back at all that you have done to complete this project. How many hours have you dedicated to it?

What have you learned about the theme?

What have you learned about the writing craft?

Look back at the list you created at the beginning of the project about why you wanted to write it. How many of those have you achieved?

How many more reasons have there been for writing it that you added to the original list? What are they?

CELEBRATE!

How will you celebrate? List ways you can reward yourself. List the people you will celebrate with.

WORKSHEETS

INTERNAL/EXTERNAL REFERENCE

Accomplishment	Negative Belief	Reality
eg, self-published a book	Everyone is doing it, not that special	Compared to the general population, only a handful of people or self-publishing. Completing a book is a big deal, having the confidence in it to put it out is even bitter
eg. Writing, work, family	I can't do everything	You are. Only *you* are expecting yourself to be perfect at it. We all have off days, days we feel like we're juggling too much. You're doing fine. It's OK to ask for help too.

Accomplishment	Negative Belief	Reality

TIME LOG

Sample Monday

Activity	Time
Morning: Breakfast Get the kids ready for school Walk the kids to school Work	 15 minutes 30 minutes 60 minutes 3.5 hours
Afternoon: Lunch with co-workers Work Pick kids up from sitters	 1 hour 3.5 hours 1 hour
Evening: Supper Chauffeuring kids Cleaning, laundry, and TV time with the hubs. Sleep	 1 hour 2 hours 3 hours not enough hours!

Monday

Activity	Time
Morning:	
Afternoon:	
Evening:	

Tuesday

Activity	Time
Morning:	
Afternoon:	
Evening:	

Wednesday

Activity	Time
Morning:	
Afternoon:	
Evening:	

Thursday

Activity	Time
Morning:	
Afternoon:	
Evening:	

Friday

Activity	Time
Morning:	
Afternoon:	
Evening:	

Saturday

Activity	Time
Morning:	
Afternoon:	
Evening:	

Sunday

Activity	Time
Morning:	
Afternoon:	
Evening:	

LIFE BALANCE WHEEL

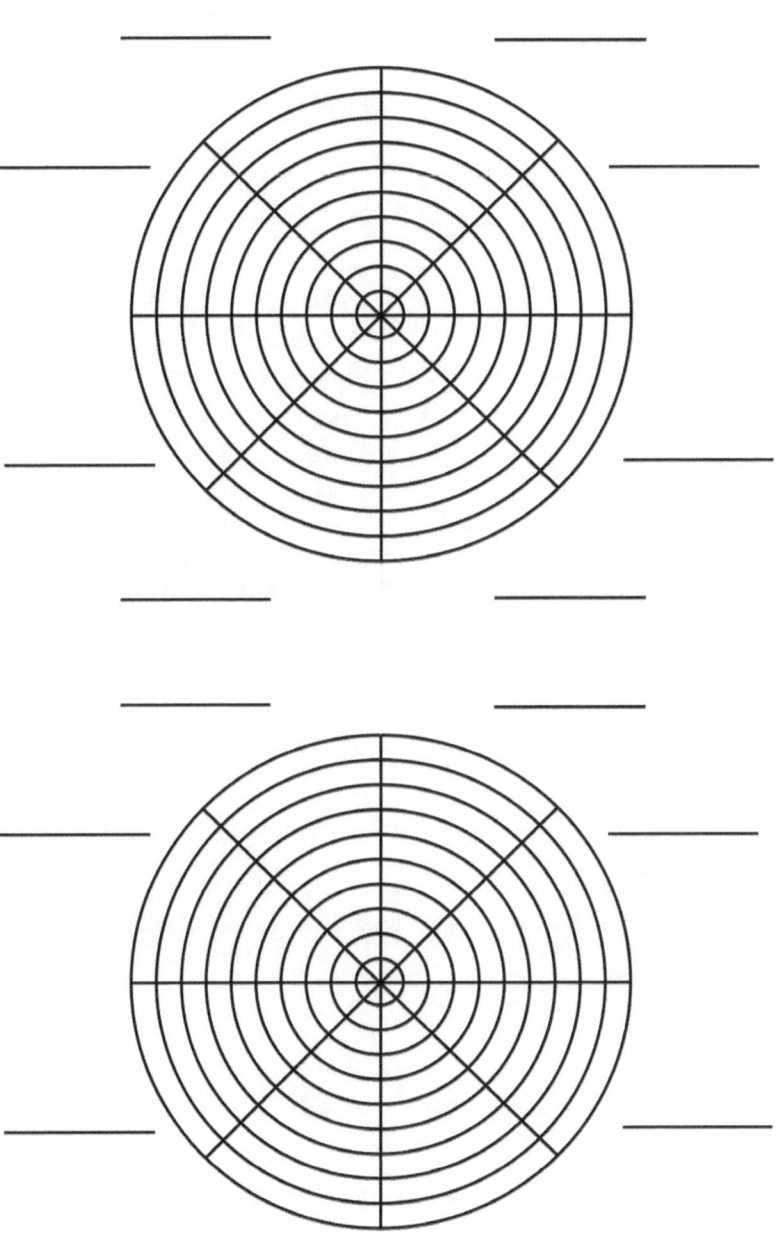

PRIORITIZATION

Urgent/Important	Important/Not Urgent
Morning Coffee Meals Sleep Taking care of emergencies Going to Work	Writing Research Writer's Group Marketing Submitting
Urgent/Not Important	Not Urgent/Not Important
Phone calls Someone at the door Paying the bills	Watching TV Playing computer games Facebook YouTube Videos Netflix

Urgent/Important	Important/Not Urgent
Urgent/Not Important	Not Urgent/Not Important

Urgent/Important	Urgent/Not Important

Not Important/Not Urgent	Not Urgent/Not Important

GOAL SETTING

Goal	Timeframe
Big Dream: New York Times Bestseller	Reached by: My lifetime
Publisher: Tor, DAW, Ace/Roc, Penguin Random House	Reached by: 5 years
Agent: Jabberwocky, Jennifer Jackson, or Sarah Megibow, or similar	Reached by: Given response times, 2 years
Submission: Full Science Fiction Manuscript with synopsis, pitch, and outline for potential series.	Submitting in: 1 year
Final edits: Polished up	Completed by: 11 months
Final feedback: Received from critique partners and beta readers.	Received by: 10 months
Third draft: Completed with all little subtleties added, polished up, and sent to critique partners and beta readers.	Completed in: 8 months
Second draft: Plot holes filled and ready for initial feedback.	Completed in: 6 months
First draft: Getting everything down on the page, including outline, side notes, and research. Aiming for 90,000 words	Completed in: 3 months.
Daily Word Count: 1,000 words a day.	

Goal	Timeframe
Big Dream:	Reached by:
Publisher:	Reached by:
Agent:	Reached by:
Submission:	Submitting in:
Final edits:	Completed by:
Final feedback:	Received by:
Third draft:	Completed in:
Second draft:	Completed in:
First draft:	Completed in: .
Daily Word Count:	

TIMELINE

Current Timeline

Summer Holidays	Back to School	Birthday	Thanksgiving	Christmas	Work Project Due
Start	Writing		Writing		End

Ideal Timeline

Start	2nd Draft	Feedback	Christmas	End
1st Draft	3rd Draft	Birthday	Edits	

Combined Timeline

Summer Holidays	Back to School	Birthday		Thanksgiving	Christmas	Work Project Due	
Start	1st Draft	2nd Draft	3rd Draft	Feedback		Edits	End

Current Timeline

_____

Ideal Timeline

_____

Combined Timeline

_____

Did you like *Blueprint for Writing Success*? Was it helpful? Please consider leaving a review on Amazon or Goodreads. All reviews are welcome and will help me reach more readers.

Don't forget to visit my website http://www.sherrypeters.com, and sign up for my newsletter which will, on occasion, have bonus writing success material and other special offers. When you sign up for my newsletter, you will receive *10 Keys to Perseverance*. As an extra extra, you will also receive the first few chapters of my other book, *Silencing Your Inner Saboteur*.

ABOUT THE AUTHOR

Sherry Peters is a Certified Life Coach who works with writers at all stages of their writing career looking to increase their productivity through pushing past the self-doubt holding them back. Sherry graduated from the Odyssey Writing Workshop in 2005 and earned her M.A. in Writing Popular Fiction from Seton Hill University in 2009. Her debut novel *Mabel the Lovelorn Dwarf* placed 1st in the 2014 Writer's Digest Self-Published e-Book Awards in the YA category. It has also been nominated for a 2015 Aurora Award, Canada's top literary award for Science Fiction and Fantasy. For more information on Sherry or her workshops, visit her website at http://www.sherrypeters.com. You can also connect with her on Facebook: https://www.facebook.com/SherryPetersSuccessCoach, and Twitter: https://twitter.com/sherry_peters

Download your free e-book copy of

Blueprint for Writing Success

today!

Purchase the print edition and receive the eBook free, in the format you want: ePub, MOBI, or PDF.

Go to www.bitlit.com to find out how.

www.ingramcontent.com/pod-product-compliance
Lightning Source LLC
Chambersburg PA
CBHW032036290426
44110CB00012B/823